Instead of the Trees

NON-FICTION BOOKS
BY J. B. PRIESTLEY

ESSAYS AND AUTOBIOGRAPHY

Midnight on the Desert
Rain upon Godshill
Delight
All About Ourselves and other Essays
  (chosen by Eric Gillett)
Thoughts in the Wilderness

Margin Released
The Moments and other pieces
Essays of Five Decades
Over the Long High Wall
Instead of the Trees

CRITICISM AND MISCELLANEOUS

The English Comic Characters
English Journey
Journey Down a Rainbow
  (with Jacquetta Hawkes)
The Art of the Dramatist
Literature and Western Man
The World of J. B. Priestley
  (edited by Donald G. MacRae)
Trumpets over the Sea

The Prince of Pleasure and
  his Regency
The Edwardians
Victoria's Heyday
The English
A Visit to New Zealand
Particular Pleasures
Outcries and Asides
English Humour

J. B. PRIESTLEY

Instead of the Trees

A Final Chapter of Autobiography

> *Men must endure*
> *Their going hence, even as their coming hither:*
> *Ripeness is all.*

HEINEMANN : LONDON

William Heinemann Ltd
15 Queen Street, Mayfair, London W1X 8BE
LONDON   MELBOURNE   TORONTO
JOHANNESBURG   AUCKLAND

First published 1977

SBN 434 60368 6

Printed in Great Britain by
Western Printing Services Ltd, Bristol

To
All my children
And grandchildren
With Love

I

The title of this book is not a bit of whimsy. But it does demand some explanation: and here it is. In the later 1930s—as I hope a few readers will remember—I published two books: *Midnight on the Desert*, a chapter of autobiography; and *Rain upon Godshill*, a further chapter of autobiography. In each of them I began by establishing myself in a certain place, and then proceeded to recall the events, opinions, thoughts, I had known during the previous twelve months or so. The first book put me in a hut I had used on a ranch in Arizona; the second began in my study on the Isle of Wight. But I had roughly planned a third chapter of autobiography; and this was to have a setting among or near the giant redwood trees of California, tranquil ancients to which I had taken a great fancy. I never began this third book because the war came and I had other work to do. I tried to forget this gap as other ideas and plans came crowding in, but I never really quite succeeded. I won't declare I was haunted by this missing trees-volume—that would be going too far—but somewhere at the back of my mind I was aware that I had planned a trio of volumes and had failed to achieve it. I still didn't like that gap. On the other hand, I no longer saw myself finding a lodging somewhere near the giant trees or indeed returning to California, not a State bent on self-improvement. So if there was to be a third volume, it would have to be, *Instead of the Trees*.

Now it has just occurred to me that we might dig a little deeper into this title. The presence of any noble old trees anywhere creates a certain atmosphere. It is tranquil, beneficent, soothing, reducing the importance and tension of the ego. They have been there much longer than we have been around, quietly putting out more branches and newer leaves, without any fuss at all,

[1]

making us seem—let's face it—rather silly. Now hardly anything could be much further removed from this quiet and gracious atmosphere than the contemporary world, the one I have to contemplate in 1976—and when too I have to do it in my old age. It is a world in which too many people don't know who they are, why they are here, and where they are going. So they fall into apathy, despair, sudden rages. It is a world that is cheerful and hopeful only in its advertisements, and is filled with salesmen desperately trying to sell something nobody really wants. (What they do want, even if it is only bread and beans, remains outside the great sales campaigns.) It switches on its TV to discover three more terrorists and five more dead bodies. It is a world that has one supreme talent—for the disastrous. So in five years it has done more to ruin a great nation, Britain, than four centuries of all-conquering tyrants could do. Can we doubt that the world we live in now is a long, long way from those trees I once thought about? So why not—for a deeper good reason—call this book, *Instead of the Trees*?

So much for the title. But now one fact has to be faced. The other two books were written by a man in his forties, when an established writer is probably at his best. Now that I have reached my eighties, I am a different creature with a very different style of life. A passage that arrives late in *Rain upon Godshill* is worth quoting here. It is really apologising for a lack of hard close thinking. (At which I am no good anyhow, being an intuitive type.)

> When I have done a bit of thinking it has been between spells of nervous anxious work in the Theatre, little but urgent political jobs of writing, speaking, organising, worries about the family health and fortunes, and of meetings, conferences, interviews, journeys, and melancholy sessions with the newspapers or the broadcast news . . .

And the political references above will not surprise people who remember 1938-9. But now comes the question. For a book of this kind, who is to be preferred, the writer who is doing too much or the one who is doing too little, the man who is trying to run a three-ring circus or the old codger who is mostly pottering about in a quiet study? I ask the question but don't know the answer, intuition failing me. But anyhow the two earlier books still exist, lively enough if beginning 'to date', and this one at least is something new. After all, what is it like to be in your eighties and a long way from your forties? Even if the average reader is much nearer his forties, he will have to move on and on, unless the twin curses of our age, tension and stress, carry him off. Notice that I say *he* and not *she*—though I am praying for plenty of feminine readers—simply because most women cope with old age much better than most men do. (I may be told that they cope with everything, except the internal combustion engine, better than men do.) Now have I made all the points I wanted to make?

Not quite, I feel. I have explained and fairly cunningly praised my title. I have suggested that while all the fuss and palaver and running around of the earlier books may be missing, *this old man* —to quote what seems to be a favourite children's chorus—may have things to say that his younger self ignored and probably didn't understand. But yes—a further point. At this time, in this age of ours, any old man, determined to express himself, has to be a very brave old boy, gallant in every totter and tremble. For the time, the age, all fashion and prejudice, are against him, as never before. He is anything but new, and it is the new that is *exciting*. (A detestable over-worked adjective, all too common, incidentally, in the Theatre.) He is no longer a man who has lived a long time and may have gained something from his experience. He is tottering out of the human race, creeping into some other species. What can we do with the old is the familiar question, with no obvious thought of shooting or smothering them but neither with any wild idea of trying to enjoy them. Grandpa or Grandma has vanished into a home, to be visited every other Sunday afternoon. They are no longer serviceable, just a problem. Yet when I was a small boy and my grandmother was living with us, looking after me when my parents had gone out for the evening, not only did we play *Beggar My Neighbour* (with me usually cheating) but she described at length her own childhood and early

[3]

II

Though never engaged in the travel-book branch of our trade, I have in fact travelled far and wide, visiting every continent (except Antarctica) more than once. And I have always gone away as a genuine traveller, making my own arrangements as I went along, and never as a tourist, the robot of some agency. But there is irony here. Going all over the world, as I have done, I have always been a bad traveller, to be put up with only by a loving wife. I am not myself a long way from home. I am vaguely apprehensive, irritable, and always ready to be disappointed. Try me with some of the most romantic place-names in the world, from Samarkand to Yucatan, and I can come up with disappointment. (Probably in a decent world I ought to have been compelled to stay at home, other people taking my place in the ship or the plane.) Looking back I realize that I did most of my far travelling in the 1930s, the 1950s and the 1960s. Looking for something quite different, the other day I found in a notebook, compiled for God knows what reason, some travel notes from the 1960s. Under 1960 itself, it simply says *America*—Nov–Dec; and what I was doing there I now have no notion. 1961 yields a richer harvest. Jan–Feb—*Luxor*, then *Paris*. July—*France*, probably the Dordogne. Sept—*Stockholm*, then *Hamburg* and *Frankfurt*. But I went elsewhere in Germany, bent on local colour for a story called *The Shapes of Sleep*. For 1962 it reads—March—*Rome*, then *Catania*. June—*Bavaria*. Oct–Nov —*Soviet Union*. That was when things looked a bit easier there, and we went as far as *Tashkent*. 1963—Jan–March—*New York* —*Mexico*—back to N.Y. Oct—*Amsterdam*, then *St-Germain-en-Laye*, where we had my eldest daughter and her husband as guests. 1964—Jan–Feb—*Morocco*. May–June—*Moscow* and *Leningrad*. Oct—*New York*. Dec—*Singapore*—as guests of same

[5]

daughter and husband. 1965—Feb—*Singapore, Penang, Hong Kong, Delhi* and *Jaipur.* July—to *Halifax, Nova Scotia,* to lecture at a drama festival, then down to *Boston,* to see friends. Oct—*Austria.* Under 1966—it simply reads *Trinidad, Guatemala, Yucatan, Mexico City.* 1967 offers us April–May—*West of Ireland,* for painting. July–Aug—New York—*Daytona Beach, Florida* (I was writing about the London Symphony Orchestra there) then *Martha's Vineyard,* to stay with friends. Under Oct we have *Paris—Villeneuve-les-Avignon, Provence, etc.* 1968—March–April—*Israel.* Sept *Frankfort* for Book Fair (first and last time). Then Oct *New York,* where the record ends.

It is also where all my visits to New York, which had begun in 1931, ended. I never wanted to see the city again. All the excitement and stimulus of my earlier visits had vanished for ever. I had seen all the sights, gone round all the excellent museums, had dined at Voisin's, at *21,* the *Four Seasons,* stayed at the *Algonquin, Hotel Pierre,* and the rest; and now I began to find the city expensive, mannerless, even sour. So I have never gone back. And not entirely without any regret. Certain Sunday mornings, always in the cool bright fall, arrive to tantalize my memory. We would walk up Fifth Avenue, enter Central Park to visit the bison there—a distant relative of mine, Jacquetta always said; and after I had reminded the bison that things were tough for all of us, we would return down Fifth Avenue, find the right restaurant, enjoy a superb dry martini, and eat too much lunch. These mornings were the best of New York to me; I admit that I have missed them.

Since 1968, when after all I was getting on a bit, if any travel record exists, I have never seen it. I know roughly where we went, but not exactly when and in what order. (I had an operation some time during this period, but have forgotten its date: a kind of travel too, that was.) What year, for instance, took us to Ceylon? It was in winter of course; and I seem to remember it was New Year's Day shortly after our arrival at our lodgings not far from Kandy. For at least a week, it rained in blanketing torrents, so nothing could be seen, except the colony of little black ants that shared our rooms. (They finally held a mass meeting under my

[6]

pillow, with delayed delegates hurrying over my face.) Before we flew out there, everybody cried, 'Oh *Ceylon*! You *are* lucky! We were there once and *adored* it.' Well, from first to last, side-trips and all, I hated it.

Even though it was the only country in which I had stones thrown at me by a gang of sullen lads, while I painted, I am not prepared to say exactly why I hated it. There was something in the atmosphere of the place that disturbed me, almost as if the abominable cruelties once practised in Kandy had poisoned the air. We met of course some pleasant hospitable people, but there was about them a noticeable lack of self-confidence and any suggestion of creative energy. They might have known in advance that the island would run into trouble, as it surely did a few years later. Certainly, as we moved around, there came moments of tranquillity and beauty, when for the time being one's heart and mind were at peace. But these were set against what seemed to me this darkly brooding atmosphere, into which a great deal of hate, both racial and social, had been spilled.

However, there was one Ceylon host who was bursting with self-confidence and creative energy and completely unaware of any hostile island atmosphere. This was the deservedly popular writer of time-and-space stories, Arthur C. Clarke, snugly at home by the sea, not far from Colombo. Clearly he could live anywhere but had enthusiastically fixed his choice on Ceylon, into which he had imported any number of new and elaborate gadgets that he insisted upon demonstrating to his bewildered but friendly guests. I think Mr Clarke is the happiest writer I have ever met. He lives just where he wants to be; he writes exactly what he wants to write; and he is successful; and I doubt, if a new planet offered itself, he would do more than pay it an exploratory visit. He is a nice chap and I liked him, and I trust he will not take offence if I suggest he is so happy there in Ceylon because he has the heart and outlook of an enthusiastic boy about sixteen. But then his Ceylon is certainly not mine.

When we were not away on trips, I used to walk into Kandy to borrow books, passing on the way groups of Singhalese girls in pretty coloured dresses who might have stepped out of an old-fashioned musical comedy. I found most of the books in the library of the British Council, but now and again I wandered into a much older library, all dust and decay and Edwardian fiction, that was like a crumbling outpost of the old Empire. But then later—oh blessed day!—we hired a car to take us up the corkscrew road, past rows of tea plantations, to what had been one of the imperial hill stations, Nuwara Eliya. It was like arriving in the England of 1910. There was a stately club, where we lunched solemnly and well, and then sat about in 1910, noticing among other things two full-sized billiard tables, which must have taken a little army of men and mules (perhaps even elephants) to hoist them up that steep winding road. Over a cup of tea, I saluted the fallen grandeur of the British Empire. But then by this time, I might have had Rudyard Kipling at my elbow, for I was becoming an imperialist years and years too late.

I don't lament the disappearance of the Empire from a British standpoint. I don't *want* an Empire. But I am not convinced, out of experience of several former colonies, that the masses all set free at last are any better off than they were under the Empire. Indeed, I think large numbers of them are worse off, being poorly governed and heavily taxed to support their independence. I not only think so but indeed have been *told so* by some poor men in various places. 'Wish the British were back,' they have muttered, well out of hearing of the middle-class intellectuals, the nationalist rebels now in power. It was the rise of these types, together with the colour nonsense following the arrival of so many white women, that brought an end to the Empire and little relief and new prosperity to the toiling masses. If people in general demand independence, then of course they must have it. But the record of that independence has on the whole been very grim, stained with more blood than that terrible Empire ever let loose. Not in Ceylon, I admit; but then Ceylon would never have known even its own history if it had not been for the laborious research there by an English civil servant; and I was not surprised to learn later that the island, idiotically governed, was turning into an ugly mess.

There were several good reasons why, in 1972, we went to

pencil sketch, which afterwards in the hotel I furiously transformed into an impressionistic angry gouache—one of my better
jobs, too, much admired.

We took the long straight roads north. (Ah—and where were
the forest roads, the arboreal villages, the ballet groups of peasant
girls perched on long carts, that I remembered from 1928? Gone
—gone for ever.) Our destination was the picturesque old town
of Kazimierz, where we would spend the night at a journalists'
rest hostel. (I began to suspect that the Ministry of Culture had
had quite enough of us by this time.) There were plenty of
journalists, of both sexes and various ages, in and around the
hostel, but not a single remark, not even a smile, came our way;
and perhaps they thought we had been planted there by the
secret police. Fortunately we were rescued from a dismal evening
by that excellent writer, Maria Kuncewicz, and her husband,
whom I had known in London during the war. They took us
round the town in the morning, when we all stared at the Vistula,
which always seems to me everywhere in Poland waiting to be
stared at. Then off we went—long straight roads again—for our
next and last one-night stand.

This was supposed to be an authors' rest house. But no authors
were chattering or carousing there. It was a very strange place—
apparently very remote (though in fact it was not far from War-
saw), run-down, melancholy, just ready for a script by a less
cheerful Chekhov. We tiptoed around, a pair of ghosts, seeing an
immense ghastly evening in front of us. But then our friend
Maria, knowing it was our last night, came to carry us off to a
goodish restaurant and some friends, and all was light, warmth,
jollity, a glimpse of a Poland that I had begun to feel had gone.
The new Poles seemed to me an unsmiling people. A Marxist
régime does not favour pleasant manners. The official hotels
where we stayed were reasonably efficient, but we never received
from one of their employees any word of welcome, any inquiry
about our comfort. The disappearance, during or just after the
war, into death or exile of the old aristocratic types and members
of the educated middle class meant a loss of the traditional gaiety,
humour, high spirits. These are probably far easier to find among

the clever successful Poles in London, Paris or New York. (Exile has long been a way of life for these people.) So though there is always Cracow, I found a return visit to Poland rather melancholy, in spite of some friendships. But on the flight home I began to wonder who were all the people who had welcomed, bought, enjoyed the Polish translation of my *Image Men*. Was it because that big comic novel laughed at almost everything?

The kind of husband I am may be briefly illustrated here. I felt rather exhausted after Poland, and said to Jacquetta, 'Travel is out. Now we go no further than Tiddington.' (The village between us and Stratford-on-Avon.) A few weeks later, I said, 'What about going to New Zealand?' (Is a maddening unpredictable husband better or worse than a dullish but reliable husband? I don't know, of course.) So we went to New Zealand and loved it; but this ambitious piece of travel is described in detail in the book I wrote about it, called—no nonsense here—*A Visit To New Zealand*. Let me make two points about that country. It is very beautiful. It isn't over-crowded. How happy I would be if it could be moved a few thousand miles nearer!

I don't object to other people gambling but I never want to gamble myself. I dislike the atmosphere it creates, over-heated both inside and outside the mind. And I always feel that while the money you lose is real, better spent on books and records, wine and cigars, the money you win is unreal, asking to be chucked away. Anyhow, I just don't need that kind of excitement. Nevertheless, our next holiday was spent in Monte Carlo. We had visited it before but had never stayed there. Why did we decide to stay there now—in February too? I can't remember. All that we were gambling on was the weather. (This needs a note. I fancy that a hundred years ago the Riviera had better weather than it has had in our time.) We were lucky in our gamble: the sun shone every day and there were no bitter winds. Being February, it was all out of season of course, but then this is what we wanted. We could even bargain a bit at the *Hermitage*, where we stayed and enjoyed a superb *table d'hôte* dinner every night. If you happen to be lucky with the weather, as we were, you can go in winter to Monte Carlo and have a delightful bourgeois holiday. (If you are not bourgeois, as I am, it is hardly worth while reading on; and anyhow what follows is chiefly meant for readers who don't know Monte Carlo.)

What is the chief attraction of this gambling place if you don't intend to gamble? To my mind it is this—that you seem to put back the time sixty-odd years. (But only in winter of course, well away from the high season.) You seem to stroll around in à lost world. The crowds, the noise, the vulgarity, the squalor, the mess, all have vanished. Streets, walks, paths, trees and grass have been cared for. Charming little shops, outposts of Paris at its best, take the place of huge glittering stores. All the waste paper and garbage have gone. There is courtesy; there is consideration. You are not being hustled and bustled from one vulgar swindle to another. You can lounge around in the open space in front of the Casino; you can go down and stare idly at the port, where the yachts of the rich are lying up; you can descend into Monaco, where, in addition to the splendid aquarium and the tropical gardens, there is another style of life, a higgledy-piggledy of cheap little shops and restaurants, where you can find—still out of season, of course—a good cheap lunch. But all this is by way of having a change, like going up to Èze or La Turbie, the kind of thing to satisfy restless wives, but for the less mobile and more sensitive male there is nothing like sauntering around, refreshed by an occasional Pernod, the cherished open spaces and well-groomed streets of Monte Carlo, moving back in time.

The principality of Monaco is a happy historical accident. We ought to have had more of them, and perhaps even now it might not be too late to save something from our detestable machine-civilization. For this 'devolution' of ours, I care nothing; it will only mean more bureaucracy and money wasted, with no real change in the quality of life. What we really need are some independent principalities like that of Monaco, where all squalid messes are abolished, where people and things are cared for, where motor traffic is largely restricted, where huge multiple stores cannot pass the frontier, where the target to be aimed at is not 1980 but 1910, and where I could go for a holiday and never leave England.

However, we didn't leave England on our next holiday, for in the middle of June, 1976, we went to the Lake District. It was a break we badly needed, for both of us had been writing continuously for an age. The Lake District was my idea, and, as we shall see, it was a bad idea. But this has nothing to do with those familiar complaints about board and lodging. In that respect we did well up there. The Sharrow Bay Country House Hotel, at Ullswater, being the darling of good-food-guiders, hadn't a room to spare for months, but its two directors, Francis Coulson and Brian Sack, very kindly invited us to share their own house for a week as paying guests, eating sumptuously at the hotel. As success stories are now so rare in our unhappy country, something must be said about Francis Coulson and Brian Sack. The latter, an affable and energetic extrovert, first arrived at Sharrow Bay as a guest but then stayed on to manage the hotel. Francis Coulson was the originating genius, both in and out of the kitchen. Cooking had fascinated him from boyhood and he had a great feeling for people, so that a dream of a different kind of hotel, more intimate and companionable, haunted him. I read an account he had set down of his first years at Sharrow Bay, when he had a mansion on his hands and hardly any money, and it reminded me of some old folk tale, in which the third son of a woodcutter ventured deep into the forest, on some dream-haunted quest, and whenever he was almost worn out, close to the dark of despair, encountered a series of little miracles, all manner of people deciding to trust him. (This, though he does not say so, was a tribute to his unusual personality.) So he was able, later with the valuable help of Brian Sack, to create the kind of hotel he wanted, with a superb kitchen, a civilized atmosphere, a sense of caring on the part of all the staff. This can be still seen and felt, but, irony being already at work, the blazing success of the enterprise is now creating its own problems. Too many people are crowding in to enjoy those dinners that Francis serves. This tends to put an edge on everything, threatening the ease and fun.

But certainly we were sorry to go, which we had to do because we had already contracted to spend the second part of our holiday in Borrowdale at the Lodore Swiss Hotel. (I had pleasant memories of Borrowdale because I had stayed there so often with Hugh Walpole, who made his home there.) Being Swiss, the Lodore is comfortable, efficient, very well managed, with any number of smiling young men to bring tea or drinks, but also being Swiss it is rather short of charm and the kitchen could do with more visits from the manager's friend, Francis Coulson. A stay there suggests we are now coming close to a classless society, for here is a four-star hotel, with fairly stiff charges, and even twenty years ago it would have been filled with obviously four-star people whereas now anybody and everybody turns up there. Do I object to this? Not at all; it makes a change; and I am merely offering, for once, a sociological note. Our bill was steep, but that was because the temperature, to my disgust, climbing to a heat wave, we drank too much. But Borrowdale, especially in the early morning and the evening, was as romantic as ever, as if designed by poets and painters in about 1830.

It was all wrong, though, up there. When I suggested we should spend our precious holiday in the Lake District, I was speaking as a lunatic, no longer in any contact with reality. I had told myself—two idiots conferring—that I had spent many happy months walking the fells and scrambling up and down the peaks, and that it was more than half a lifetime since I had revisited these delectable places. I was of course quietly out of my mind. I had forgotten that I was now in my eighties—and over-weight at that. All I could do now was to sit in a car and take my miserable share of the fells and peaks through its windows. I felt like a melancholy exile, which indeed is what I was—from the happy land of youth. When I wasn't feeling melancholy, I itched and burned with irritation. Why? Because although this was only June and not August, ten thousand other cars were hooting and groaning there.

Certainly the two of us were also sitting in a car, groaning a little if not hooting. And if we were there, why shouldn't all the other people be there? This is a rational question, and like so many rational questions it leaves heart and mind dissatisfied, refusing to supply an answer. What we really *feel* on these occasions is that we have a right to be there because, in ways unspecified, we are *different* from all those other people. The Lakes want us—and don't want all this mob, turning Grasmere into one of the outer suburbs of Blackpool. And Keswick—never a favourite, unlike Penrith—was a baking confusion of fuss and wrong turnings. But here I must remind the English reader that in the latter half of June, 1976, the temperature rose and rose and a heat wave descended upon us. I had prepared myself for constant rain—to the extent of taking Trollope's political novels and two packs of Patience cards—but not of course for this merciless inferno, which made even car travel exhausting and removed all height, dignity and variety of tone from all the fells and peaks, and left me without the least desire to try a paint or two. In fact, after spending too much on drink, to renew the mind as well as the body, I longed to go home. But the cursed heat followed me there, so that I spent day after day half-dressed in curtained rooms, unable to work or even think, feeling at times as if I had died and entered some stale warm Limbo, beyond the reach not only of friends but even of publishers and play agents. Of course I had often visited distant places much hotter than this, but there I was visitor, with a bag to be packed soon, whereas now I was at home, where it used to rain or bring fresh cool mornings and I could do some thinking and working. The few people I encountered in this Limbo said that my holiday had done me good, chiefly because I had a red face, so much crimson indignation and half-bottled fury.

Even so I brought away a precious memory, that of a perfect hour. We had taken packed lunches because I wanted to explore the Langdale region, where I had once rented a furnished cottage, fifty-five years ago. Deciding to eat somewhere near Dungeon Ghyll we worked our way up the valley, which was mostly cars, heat and fuss. At last we arrived, hot and thirsty, at the old hotel up there, and we had its cool ancient tap room to ourselves. We drank that mixture of gin and draught bitter which we insist upon calling 'Dog's Nose', though I believe the traditional drink is a spiced hot mixture. The nose of our dog was wonderfully cool and refreshing. So was the room itself, with its fine old woodwork, its distance from all heat and fuss and internal combustion engines, its quiet, its tranquillity, its suggestion of taking yesterday, today and tomorrow all in one long, easy look. We had it to ourselves. We quietened down and expanded there, relaxed in body and larger in spirit. It might have been Chesterton's Inn at the End of the World, and indeed for an hour that's what it was. It was old, had known so many very different years, and yet it welcomed us. It made progress look like an overheated daft perturbation and idiotic turmoil, with everybody rushing towards frustration. We are now taxed to hell and gone, just for more and more of that sweating imbecility, and not a single minister and his advisers are taking our money and toiling to provide us with more places like the tap room of the old hotel at Dungeon Ghyll. We rest and are quiet for an hour, just where the past meets the present, and it is like a little miracle, which even the Arabs can't buy. For about sixty unmeasured and silent minutes, we had a holiday.

III

For this section I ought to borrow an early title of Arnold Bennett's—*The Truth about an Author*. I didn't discover until the other day that I have a first edition of this work, published in 1903, after being serialized in *The Academy*. Bennett begins in a manner that he would certainly have rejected twenty years later:

> I, who now reside permanently on that curious fourth-dimensional planet which we call the literary world; I, who follow the incredible parasitic trade of talking about what other people have done, who am a sort of public weighing-machine upon which bookish wares must halt before passing from the factory to the consumer; I, who habitually think in articles, who exist by phrases; I, who seize life at the pen's point and callously wrest from it the material which I torture into confections styled essays, short stories, novels, and plays; who perceive in passion chiefly a theme, and in tragedy chiefly a 'situation'; who am so morbidly avaricious of beauty that I insist on finding it where it is not; I, in short, who have been victimized to the last degree by a literary temperament, and glory in my victimhood, am going to trace as well as I can the phenomena of the development of that idiosyncrasy from its inception to such maturity as it has attained . . .

All of which, I am afraid, is a model of How Not To Write. But Bennett matured late—though well—and I have always felt sorry that he had only twenty-eight more years left. I well remember the morning, in sight of Tahiti, when the news of his death came on the ship's radio. He was one of those men—kind and generous, doing nobody any harm—whose luck suddenly begins to run out in all directions, as if victims of some doom pronounced behind the veil. We were never friends, just literary acquaintances, but I was happy to deliver the centenary lecture on him at Stoke, broadcasting it too. I had re-read his *Imperial Palace*, not received as well as he had hoped (the luck was already going), and regretted I hadn't made more of it after my first reading. We have all been sentenced, early or late, and might be pleasanter to one another, sitting in Death Row.

Well now, after seventy-odd years since his *Truth about an Author*, I shall in this section follow the same path. I don't know how truthful he was—the manner and style he chose wouldn't be any great help there—but I shall certainly try to tell the truth. (After all, he was only about thirty-six and self-conscious, while I am eighty-one, a bit mannered no doubt, but not really caring a damn.) Now in my piece on *The Happy Dream*, to which we shall come, I begin by referring to daydreams, waving them away, and suggesting I have never indulged in them myself. I cheat a little there, but only a very little, because the only daydream was a very modest one and I was still in my teens when it took possession of me. This was from about 1912 to August 1914, when a world ended.

I was living at home in Bradford then, and I was a junior clerk in a wool office. (I had a letter a few years ago saying in effect, 'You can't imagine what it's like being a clerk in an office from 9 to 5 every day'; to which I replied that I could easily recall working in an office from 9 to 6.30, with a long Saturday morning thrown in and just two days' holiday at Christmas and Easter.) Even so, I was writing all the time: verse, not good; shortish pieces, comic sketches and the like; and very pompous articles, weighing a ton, and signed *J. Boynton Priestley*. These, except the verse, I sent off to editors, and usually they came back. (I had a friend who papered his cottage with rejection slips.) However, now and again, they squeezed into print, and I earned ten or fifteen shillings, even a guinea one time.

As yet there wasn't even the skeleton of a living here. How did I begin to write my way out of that wool office? And this is when and where the daydream—the only one I ever had—haunted me. Did I dream of going to London and discovering fame and fortune there? I did not. (And please remember I was a provincial lad aged eighteen or nineteen.) I would just as soon have imagined myself playing Hamlet at the Lyceum Theatre or conducting the London Symphony in the Queen's Hall. The London-fame-and-fortune ploy never occurred to me. My single though recurring daydream wasn't only on a very much smaller scale but also wasn't entirely beyond the bounds of possibility. This was due to the fact that in those days wages and fees might be low, so was the cost of living. (I insist on making a point here. It is my experience that with a high cost of living come tension, strain and stress, envy and malice, and trouble all round.) If, I told myself, I could earn a fairly steady five or six pounds a month—by writing, of course—I would walk out of that wool office for ever.

Moreover, I would settle down on my own for a few years. I knew there were stoutly-built moorland cottages that might be rented at about a shilling a week, for various friends of mine used such cottages simply for week-ends and I had stayed in them. No mod. con. of course; it would mean fetching water from the nearest pump and having only lamplight; but what did that matter when at nineteen you were reaching your heart's desire? Yes, once outside that wool office, I would settle down, a professional writer, in one of those cottages. I would leave home; not because I was unhappy there—I was as reasonably contented as a lad my age could be—but because I felt that a professional writer should have his own place, all the better if close to the moors, with long lark-sweetened walks for inspiration. And this was the height, breadth and depth of my daydream, with not the merest glimmer of fame and fortune coming into it.

I never thought about London except as the place where some editors lived. This is not as surprising as it might seem. We were regional folk before the First War. Of course some of us had visited London—I am not thinking about business men now—just as these days people take a look at Madrid or Stockholm. But the West Riding was where we lived and had our being. I never remember my father, a schoolmaster and well-read, ever bothering about a London newspaper. His paper was the *Yorkshire Observer*, published in Bradford. (And I remember parts of

H. M. Tomlinson's *Sea and Jungle* being serialized in it—superb reading.) However, my father might occasionally take a look at the *Manchester Guardian*, just as I did. Even our well-to-do women didn't go rushing up to London to do their shopping, for Bradford's Darley Street—very different then from what it is now—was good enough for them. Our cultural life wasn't narrow and provincial, even if most of us looked and sounded as if we were. Great music and famous performers came to us; we were well provided with drama and variety; we had an excellent Arts Club, and painters, with the Dales so near, were working all round us. The truth is, Bradford from 1911–1914 gave me more than Cambridge did from 1919–1922. True, in this last year I left for London and didn't return North except for holidays. But then everything was different by that time. I knew I could earn a living, in or near London, by writing—to keep a family too—and that is why I refused a number of safe academic jobs, a fact that some academics might bear in mind.

(Recalling my various attitudes towards London, the record would run as follows. I was closest to London, both in body and spirit, during the 1930s and 1940s. I began to move away from it, on both levels, in the '50s and '60s, gradually losing the affection I had felt before and during the Second War. During these '70s the city looked different and worse. It became a noisy, over-crowded, expensive place with a traffic problem (too many delivery vans) it hadn't the guts to solve. Many good little West End shops had vanished; there were few theatres I wanted to visit; I could provide myself with music at home; the big art exhibitions were always too crowded; favourite restaurants were closing or pricing themselves clean out of my particular market; and though there were some friends left—and too many had died—we wanted to meet, it was often better to see them down here in the country. Unlike Jacquetta, I wasn't a member of a single committee; I had been quite ruthless about that; so only when business with publisher or agent called me, did I climb reluctantly those steps into Albany. I wanted to stay at home. And yet—and yet—not only to be fair but also to stop grumbling —there were—and are—heightened moments when I stared at night across the river and the South Bank was all lit up, and enchantment returned again, and I felt I had only to cross a bridge, and beneath the misty illuminations Shakespeare and Mozart might be there to welcome me. A great city of illusion and enchantment had come back—at the last possible moment.)

No large golden daydreams of fame and fortune were coming my way during the years 1922–25. I had two infant daughters (now the mothers of splendid families themselves) and a young wife doomed to go in and out of hospital because she was trying to fight—and in vain, at last—an inoperable cancer. Between visits to hospitals or hiring nurses, I had to stick grimly at my desk, determined to meet all bills without borrowing a cent, though occasionally, in spite of bouts of nervous exhaustion, finding in the sheer necessity of getting down to work a certain anodyne. (And here I must pay a tribute to the women doctors of the Royal Free Hospital, where, after some rather callous and stupid medical treatment, my wife, still in her twenties and dying by inches, was eased at last towards her final passing in the autumn of 1925.) It was during this dark time, when I was compelled by every circumstance to drive myself to keep hard at work, both to pay the bills and to try to forget what was happening, that I formed the habit of writing too much and resting too little, with results to which I shall return later.

Even when this time had gone and I was beginning a new life, I drove on and on. So, for example, in the later 1920s, I would spend a day writing essays and criticism, and then go back to my study after dinner and there write chapter after chapter of a rather fantastic long tale that belonged to the night: I called it *Benighted*, though in New York and Hollywood, where it was well received, it was known as *The Old Dark House*. But I was already planning an unfashionably long novel, though I knew my publishers regarded any such thing with disfavour. It would be a return in some sort to the old tradition of the big picaresque story, which had always fascinated me. It would also offer me a holiday from reality. (I can stand up to reality—and indeed had been sharply compelled to do so—for there had been the war and then that dark time afterwards.) I would write a long crowded tale that would be in effect a fairy story set against a fairly realistic background. And I would call it—against everybody's advice—*The Good Companions*, something I have never been allowed to forget, though I have done better things. It must be thoroughly understood that I never had 'a bestseller' in mind. I really don't think like that. After all I don't know what people want—they don't know themselves—and what I am sure of is what I want to do myself, I who have to spend so much time and energy on the thing.

Surely a pattern is now emerging? I began, still a junior clerk, spending much of my spare time writing—in various forms—and cherishing the one daydream I ever had, no golden vision. Clearly I was an unambitious youth. And I have never been an ambitious man. I have never spent ten minutes planning a literary career. (Oddly enough, it is chiefly the poets who have been the careful career-planners—Yeats and Eliot, for example; perhaps Auden and Spender.) But after Cambridge, I acquired the habit of working hard and continually, driven partly by circumstances, partly by a puritan work-ethic I owed to my upbringing, partly because I always seemed to have a lot of good ideas—though of course some of them may have been stupid—beginning to be caught and set down on paper. These were never hack jobs; even during the worst time, they never were; and by the time the 1930s arrived, I was comfortably off. But even on that ranch in Arizona (see *Midnight on the Desert*), though I might be out riding or playing tennis all afternoon, I was usually working in the morning and early evening. The pattern is now here, and it is a bad one. I am writing too much: I am idling and brooding too little.

However, I must put up one line of defence. Not being a handsome charmer (in my sex always spoilt from boyhood), I felt from the first, being no treat at all, I had to justify my existence. Nothing to look at, but all the same, very entertaining: that was my style, from school onwards. And then there was something else, and to understand it you have to be very well-acquainted with the West Riding of Yorkshire, where I was born and brought up. This is no place for flower-like types born to blush unseen. Its typical society is rigorous, demanding, challenging, not unlike a rough sea voyage. A good West Riding man never ignores or tries to move away from any challenges. He responds almost at once, sometimes indeed before they have been made, when he just smells them in the air. I don't say I am one of the more ferocious of these instant responders—some men up there could bite your head off after a two-minute argument about cricket—but my worst enemy—and I have had some stinkers—couldn't fairly accuse me of bolting at the sight of a challenge. *Try me— and you'll see!* I don't think I ever said that to anybody, but that is often what I meant.

So all through my writing life there has been this challenge-and-response element. It could be put bluntly like this. You'll nivver mak' a writer, Jacky Priestley. *Oh—won't I? Well, watch out!* You can write these essays and so forth, but you'll never manage a novel. *That's what you think! Just you wait!* Novels no doubt, but not plays. *Don't be too sure! I've already written two.* Some chaps are doing well out of this broadcasting. But not you. *Not yet, but I'll be on to it when the time's ripe.* This dialogue must not be taken seriously of course. I may be insufferable, but not *that* insufferable. But the challenge-and-response element was nearly always there, and if it wasn't I would amuse myself writing anything that tickled my fancy at the moment, indulging myself in a kind of aesthetic indolence, playing rather than working. (Left alone, when not responding, I tend to be lazy-minded, passing hours and hours with pipe tobacco and desultory reading. Though even this last served me in its turn, as in *Literature and Western Man.*) However, to snap myself out of self-indulgent ease, I would from time to time deliberately create my own challenges.

I did this by offering myself hard nuts to crack. The kernels can be found in my best plays and novels. In these I am quite original, not imitating anything done before. This fact is largely ignored, chiefly because I am not eccentric, am fairly sensible, don't go in for self-advertisement (unlike Shaw, who never missed a chance), and have never asked my wife and friends to regard me as a genius, which I am not. But even so, a close examination of my work will prove that from time to time I have written some plays and novels quite markedly different from any other plays and novels. They may be better, they may be worse; that is not for me to decide; I only say the best of them are definitely original. And they were a response to my challenges to myself. But knowing what I do now, I think I would have done better, right from the beginning, if I had issued much bigger and more demanding challenges to myself. Here I am no longer thinking of actual pieces of work but of a complete life-style.

Honesty shall take over. I believe I would have been wiser to have entertained some large golden daydreams of fame and fortune, right from the beginning. I would have done better then to have been far more ambitious, ready to plan a career. After that I could have been less easy and self-indulgent along the way, keeping quiet when I was not responding to definite challenges. Looking back, I realize now that while I have had a fair number of enemies, I myself have been the worst of them. I have written too much, far too much for my own good. For years I have been standing in my own light, overshadowing my better self. So I have been often ignored or brushed aside by people who, if a talent for writing is accepted as a test, are just about fit to clean my type-writer. So again, time after time I have been described—with no malice intended—as a *man of letters*, who has occasionally pro-duced plays and novels, probably mediocre letters-man jobs. Now I declare emphatically that I take no pride whatever in being called a *man of letters*—ugh!—a term applied, especially in my younger days, to any number of book-sodden dreary old hacks. It suggests at once somebody who is boring and out-of-date and can be ignored by eager young readers. Now while I am freely admitting my mistakes—which seem to multiply in recollection the older one gets—I must also stand up here and shout, *I am not that kind of man at all.*

However cluttered up and smudged the record might be, due to the fact that I like to be writing something and cannot resist an idea that amuses me, I am essentially at heart a creative writer. I am either that or nothing, and I can easily prove I am not a nothing. Whatever else I have written, I have to be considered first in terms of my plays and novels and the vast distances they have travelled. Not all of them, of course, because some of them have been written slackly and move too easily over the surface of this life. See!—I confess it. But while I don't pretend to be one of the great primary writers, most of them would have to confess it too. Some academics cannot help assuming that creative writers should be passing examinations, with so many credits for good work, so many black marks for bad. Fortunately the world outside their lecture rooms ignores this pedantic procedure.

When I have in mind the best of my plays and novels, I find they are far from being old-fashioned and out-of-date. They have a strange trick of catching up with life and suddenly becoming topical. This is most easily discovered in the Theatre with revivals, where I have been able to watch the faces of the young, alight with interest, even excitement. The play—it might be *Time and the Conways* or *An Inspector Calls*—may have been written before they were born, but it has come to life for them, sometimes in productions of no great merit in themselves. On the other hand, the young rarely reveal themselves as novel-readers, if only because they don't like writing letters. (The Post Office itself is hardly enthusiastic about letters, though reserving its black hatred for parcels—books too, perhaps.) As for novels becoming topical—as I write this I am waiting eagerly for the publication in one volume of my longest (and best) novel, *The Image Men*. This huge comedy, satirical though not sour, ironically explores the whole image-making business, and it is more topical, immediate, up-to-the-minute, at this time *than when I wrote it*. Reality has caught up with it.

Comic fiction has its dangers. Ordinary readers, outside literary fashion, are not against it, but some people who regard themselves as critics scorn it. I was reminded of this when I was visited, a short time ago, by an Indian graduate who was preparing a thesis on my work. Wasn't I worried, he asked, that my comic fiction would set me apart from serious criticism. I said that all manner of things had me worried nowadays, but not this particular danger. Better novelists had been dismissed as mere entertainers long before my time. If there was a grand central tradition,

[26]

I went on, in English fiction it was the Comic, from Fielding and Sterne onwards. I was trying to work in that tradition while at the same time revealing the kind of life going on all round me. If that provides entertainment, well and good, but any reader who can find nothing else there is a fool, fit subject for comedy himself. Think of provincial high jinks in *Festival at Farbridge*, of broadcasting in *Low Notes on a High Level*, of the rival Arts Councils in *Sir Michael and Sir George*, and of almost everything waiting to be laughed at in my giant pet, *The Image Men*.

Notice the way I have come in this piece. I begin by blaming myself; I continue by defending myself; I end—inevitably—by praising myself. We all do it, though most of us do it when nothing much is at stake: only a select and highly-publicised few do it while the possible ruin of their country stares them in their brassy faces. I will make such amends as I can conjure up by giving some advice to any young writer at the outset of a literary career, while reminding him (or her of course, but let us assume this) that he was born too late to live in a literary society; that books, apart from paperbacks screaming with scandal, are on their way out; that money and fame will come first to his cousin, now appearing regularly in *Hi-Pussy!* on TV; that publishers, agents, reviewers, even his aunts, will all be dubious; that the sight of all that blank typing paper will make Monday morning hideous; that he cannot look forward to any golden handshake, any perks and fat pension, and if he does have a success at last, then the taxman will half murder him.

Advice to a young writer. First, do as I say, not as I have done. Don't be afraid of a few large golden daydreams. After you have enjoyed them, settle down to plan some sort of career. Don't drift along, too much at ease, waiting for a challenge to turn up. Then write too little rather than too much; keep your product in short supply; make them wait for your next contribution; play hard to get. Don't dodge about too much; keep to the same kind of thing, so that you fit neatly into Eng. Lit. pigeonholes and won't be ignored. Never oppose the Establishment, which after all may have a prize waiting for you. Refuse immediately anything that might turn you into a public figure associated with unpopular

IV

Why not a section, as honest as I can make it, on Old Age? A lot of people have told us how they are enjoying—or have enjoyed their old age. I am not one of these complacent ancients. I detest being old. I can't settle down to make the most of it— whatever that may be—but resent almost every aspect of it. There is still in me a younger man, trapped, struggling to get out. It is rather as if I were press-ganged at a stage door, dragged in to submit to *old-man make-up*, and then pushed on the stage to play an objectionable character part. For instance, I am increasingly fussy about engagements and arrangements and time-tables. Meanwhile, there is a self that is aware of all this fussiness and deplores it. This confirms my opinion that in old age we are compelled to play a bad character part, not belonging to our essential and enduring self. We are out there, facing an intimate audience, making fools of ourselves.

Anyhow, I am living at the wrong time. Had I been born even forty or fifty years earlier, I might have enjoyed going on so long. But now, it seems to me, old age is a liability without the ghost of an asset. The ripe experience of us who are old is now not of any value. It may be we have no wisdom, but then is anybody looking for wisdom? We have no longer anything important to contribute. (But then sometimes I feel that those still in their prime haven't very much, with so many huge problems around and so many inadequate solutions.) There have been civilizations of a sort in which the aged have been expected to climb a mountain and vanish for ever in its mists and snow. Perhaps that mountain is still with us—existing in the inner space of our juniors, hoping to forget us.

Certainly if I played my part properly, I would have it easier. I mean by this a fireside-dressing-gown-dotage existence, behind a huge beard garnished with crumbs and egg. But I don't live that kind of life at all. I keep on writing in the morning and early evening, though finishing sooner than I used to do. I am still involved in various kinds of business, even using the long-distance telephone when I feel I can afford to use it. I am down to breakfast at nine, dressing-gowned though, and then after dictating a few letters (if necessary) I go upstairs to shave and dress, usually about 10.30. I come down and work until about 12.50. Unless it is raining I take a short walk in the afternoon, rarely seeing other walkers, only cars, and then I read or do a little work until tea. I am at work again, roughly between 5.30 and 6.30—only an hour but an hour of actual writing, and not thinking about writing. (I do that at teatime.) Then I go up for a leisurely shower and a change of clothes, not anything much nattier but just a change. Bed about 11.30. Read until about one o'clock, sometimes later. Unless we have house guests, Saturday's programme is much the same. But I am leaving out the social side, dining out or having people in to dine.

But I have a point to make about all this carry-on. Because I am old, almost everything mentioned above demands both effort and patience. Nothing runs itself. What—even getting dressed or going to bed? Certainly. They are both workouts. I don't say tremendous efforts are involved, but there are no easy routines here, nothing accomplished while thinking about something else. I can have a little wrestling match just getting into a pair of trousers. Just coping with the mere arrangements of ordinary living, there must continually be an exercise of will. To get by from 9 in the morning until midnight I use enough willpower to command an army corps. Is there no fun along the way? Yes, of course; but I wish there was more—and much less effort. Any serene old age is still well out of sight. I am in a fair way to become one of the really grumpy old meanies, cackling at the deaths of acquaintances. But of course not of friends.

Here the loss is hideous, really hard to bear. We begin to outlive friendship on a desolating scale. I take one example. Just over fifty years ago, a large group of us, including some famous literary figures, used to meet in a Fleet Street pub to drink and air our wit. Only two of us are left, the other survivor being J. B. Morton, that glorious wild humorist, *Beachcomber*; and we have lately exchanged letters, and it has been like two small ships flashing signals across a huge darkness. Whatever other people may say, to me it is no joke growing old. Not only do friends vanish, leaving blank spaces, but sometimes the news can be terrible: two of the closest friends I ever had, man and wife, both died horrible lingering deaths. It is true that in the end you grow a kind of carapace, to protect what store of feeling you have left, so that I turn a lacklustre eye on those official appeals for help that come, sometimes quite alone, through the letterbox. I am not yet a very mean old man, but I am moving in that direction. I view with increasing distaste those guests who can leave an inch or so of good wine in their glasses.

A familiar figure, if only in legend, is the old man who sits by the fire, hour after hour, recalling past triumphs. I never find myself doing this, and I suppose I have had my share of triumphs on a writer's modest scale. I am more apt to poke around in my recollections and then discover the mistakes I have made. Here is one of the greatest, a warning perhaps to other but younger writers. It is this. I have spent too much time doing what came naturally to me—writing—when I ought to have turned aside from it far more often to do other things. I could have been digging and planting in the garden. I ought to have started painting much earlier, not leaving it until my sixties. I could have followed Jacquetta's example, enjoying natural history and being knowledgeable about it: my ignorance is appalling. Instead of leaving the piano alone, except for some very rare strumming, I might at least have kept my fingers in practice. Astronomical discoveries and speculations fascinate me—think of those *black holes*!—but I have made no serious study of the science. Indeed, I haven't made a serious study of any subject removed from literature and history. When I was much younger I read a lot of philosophy, but as soon as the linguistic fellows arrived, they turned me off, and I have stayed off ever since. This is a disgraceful record, and if I am now a dissatisfied grumpy old man, it serves me right.

One thing has happened. I have lived long enough now to understand why some people disliked or despised me. And this is new. I am not going so far as to say I ought to have been disliked or despised. What I am saying is that understanding has now replaced furious resentment and indignation. Those people, I see, had some justification. I catch a glimpse of their point of view. But why this change? I think it is because now I am no longer in love with myself, as I must have been once. I may still have a fairly good opinion of myself, as indeed I think we all ought to have. (The mind of any man who really hates or despises himself is a disaster area, always bringing bad news.) But the old self-love affair has vanished, and some measure of understanding has taken its place. Now, recalling various past episodes, I tell myself I asked for trouble.

But how must I account for certain feelings? Do they belong to insight or are they lumps of octogenarian prejudice? Let me take one example. I can't help feeling—even while I try to check myself—that there is now in our world a marked absence of great sure talent. Tremendous ability, in all departments, is hard to find. We look for giant figures, but where are they? (I agree they may be hidden among the labs and behind the paraphernalia of the sciences, just waiting to announce some astounding conclusions.) It is as if we had now created an atmosphere—compounded out of pollution, stress, too many people—in which gigantic personages can't find sufficient nourishment. We are in the dwarf, zombie, robot, business. And even if we are not, we are certainly crowding ourselves out, possibly with not enough space for high excellence to lift its head. This reminds me of an idea that occasionally disturbs me. Suppose there is only so much genius, great talent, high excellence, to go round, so that the more and more people there are at a given time, the poorer and thinner the distribution is, with never a ration to nourish a giant. Thus in the year 2000 anything but the dreariest mediocrity might be unthinkable. Already our political ideologists, bent on rejecting quality in education, are pushing us in that direction.

If all this seems rather harsh, it comes from some bitter reflections. I have suggested already that this is a bad time for any approach to or arrival at old age. We are well out of fashion. But that isn't all, not by a long nasty piece of chalk. Just suppose, reader, you are in your eighties and a grandfather with a large family. You are no treat to look at or to listen to; play no games, no longer drive a car, can't venture on long walks; really a poor old thing. But at any other time but this snarling brute of a time, you could at least *be generous*. That is your role—good old lavish grandpa! To play the role you must be on the spot—and not in some remote taxhaven—and if you are on the spot nowadays, then you can't sustain the role. Most of your money is ruthlessly removed from you—we are in Britain of course—because you are under a government that is only generous, extravagant, carefree about money, to and with and for *itself*. Its attitude towards you is that of a mangle towards damp clothes. Most of what you earn belongs to it, even if necessary before you know what you have been earning. Before you can work out what to give your grandchildren for Christmas, a host of people are on your back, with their hands reaching down to your pockets, removing money that might as well be flung out of the window.

Bitter—eh? Certainly I am bitter, if only because I am old and *I have had enough of it*. I have paid my whack, and now we who are really old—all of us frustrated grandfathers—should at last be *let off* and not badgered, bullied and mulcted right to the edge of the grave. Some years ago, I called at No. 11 Downing Street to appeal to a former Chancellor of the Exchequer. I suggested to him that any man over seventy-five should pay no income tax at all *on earned income*. This would cost the government very little, and would make life much easier for a number of old people, some of them of considerable distinction and still earning their living. (A few jobbing gardeners possibly, but probably far more artists and scientists.) We had a drink and he listened to me attentively. Finally he said he agreed with me in principle, but the reform would be difficult to administrate, if only because all Civil Service pensions were treated as *earned income*. (Collapse of stout party!) These same pensions, I believe, are now to be protected against any erosion by inflation. Nobody can say our government doesn't look after itself and its own.

Some of us would like to catch a glimpse of the State wearing the same smiling face. We are of course mostly old and short of temper.

At all times, I seem to remember, I have never played the part a good social life-style has expected me to play. This is certainly true now, when I ought to be a serene and sweet old man, preferably with plenty of snow-white hair and a beautiful beard, not half-bald, clean-shaven and with horrid bags under the eyes. It is, I repeat, the fault of that younger man, trapped by the ruthless years, and still trying to get out. He must be responsible for a snarling graceless old age. And now I have just remembered something I wrote in *Margin Released* about fifteen years ago. Here it is:

> ...Sometimes I wonder if I was unlucky in my birthplace. Further south I might now be called *maître* and, wearing a skullcap, receive homage every Thursday night and Sunday afternoon. Further north and east, clear-eyed solemn maidens might bring flowers to the house on my birthday. Unfortunately we have no sensible English equivalent of these signs of public esteem, except those pats on the head and shoulder from the Establishment, meant for better or worse men, not for me...

But now let us be clear about all this. I would be embarrassed by gatherings of admirers or maidens bringing flowers, and have firmly declared my lack of interest in Establishment honours, traditionally unwelcome in my profession. All I ask in fact is to be let alone, to cope as best I can—and in private—with the weaknesses, the constant demands on willpower, of old age. But, in a bad sense, I am not left to myself. As I have already declared, I am increasingly badgered, bullied and mulcted. I am recognized officially only as a pip that must be made to squeak, so that the state can make more and more daft investments. I am not an aged man who has done some service but a milch cow. And so, though no disciple of Dylan Thomas, I refuse to go gentle into that good night. You might say I alternate between a general grumpiness and downright anger. And clearly there are better ways of spending one's final years.

However, there is something else, much more impersonal, that ought to be said. A State that taxes ferociously while spending freely itself is a danger. It wears two very different masks: one is Dick Turpin, the other is Santa Claus. Wearing Turpin it confiscates so much that a man may earn a good income and yet have little opportunity to be charitable himself, as he could be forty years ago. As Santa Claus, spending money it has never earned itself but only grabbed, it may be regarded by millions as the fount from which all blessings flow. Increasingly it becomes more and more powerful, a threat to the ancient liberties of its subjects. The sheer size and weight of its bureaucratic machinery become daunting. Moreover, what it does tends to be expensive, clumsy, ungracious. Even when I was a socialist I was never a State socialist, believing—rather vaguely, I must confess—in a common ownership belonging to cooperatives, public corporations, and the like. The State, in my book, was always a big clumsy bully. To allow it to confiscate more and more, to spend more and more on itself, to acquire more and more power, seemed to me even then a disaster. And this I feel even more strongly now, when any chances I may have to be compassionate and generous are rapidly dwindling, when harder work only attracts larger and more ruthless demands, when the very idea of a *windfall*, once such a treat in my profession, can now be dismissed. And if, on top of all this, the very notion of a liberal freedom-loving democracy is shrinking and in peril, then I can hardly be blamed if I alternate, as I have already declared, between a general grumpiness and downright anger. It is well beyond a joke to live so long, only to become the victim of fanatical ideologists, the very people I have always detested. Certainly I could think of far better ways of spending my final years.

V

In this section, still keeping to the last eight years or so, I propose to consider the books I have published. This is an unusual task for a writer, unless he or she is writing a very full autobiography. We are rarely able to look at books *from the inside*, as the author sees them. I feel that no harm but some good may come of this, especially as many of these books—though no 'bestsellers'—have encountered a large number of readers.

We begin in 1968 with the publication of my longest novel, 300,000 words, *The Image Men*. It was brought out—a grievous mistake, I now realize—in two separate volumes, and so hadn't then the impact it ought to have had. (It can now be read in one volume, without the text having been cut at all.) It attracted a good deal of loose easy praise, which left me as it found me, except for a conclusion by Iris Murdoch, no easy praiser, who said, 'A very clever and funny book with real people in it.' And that, I beg to add, is just what it is. Not so long ago, I sat down to tackle it simply as a reader and it delighted me. (I was so lost in it that I thought how clever Professor Saltana and Dr Tuby were with their impressive image nonsense, clean forgetting that I had invented it all.) It now became my first favourite among all my novels.

But at a time when reading was hardly very patient, why did I risk making this novel so long, a formidable lump of fiction? There were two reasons for this. First, I needed a number of targets for my (amiable) satire. I took my two image experts, Saltana and Tuby, into academic life, the media and films, advertising and big business, and politics. This asked for a broad long canvas. The second reason was more self-indulgent. I was so fondly attached to my two middle-aged heroes, Saltana and Tuby, that I was reluctant to let them go, feeling I could have gone on writing about them for years. (They are of course parts of myself, suitably enlarged.) I fancy that it is this affection that prevents the satire from turning sour, while it also adds a certain depth and realism to their sexual relationships, better done here than in any of my earlier novels. Moreover, I was able to keep the huge tale more or less all in one key, which I had failed to do in *Bright Day*, even though I am still proud of that novel's feeling for youth and its artful time-shifts. So *The Image Men* remains—and must remain, for I can no longer write fiction on that scale—my own first favourite. Alas that its sheer size will not enable it to follow *Angel Pavement* and *Bright Day* into the Everyman Library list of what it takes to be modern classics! Still, *The Image Men* shines the brightest in my memory and my heart.

With this giant fiction behind me, I decided to turn to social history, fully illustrated too, and published in turn *The Prince of Pleasure*, its subject the Regency, *The Edwardians*, and then *Victoria's Heyday*, based on the 1850s. In spite of their numerous illustrations, which I enjoyed selecting, these were far from being hack jobs in the coffee-table-book trade. The text was not a mere excuse for the pictures. It was thoroughly researched and had to cover politics, the arts and sciences, the lives of both the great and the humble. I had always had a taste for and a fair knowledge of history, especially social history; and so these books were something more than a respite from writing novels and plays. They satisfied a certain old longing in me, far more important than the money they brought me, money I was in no urgent need of. But what was equally important was that they brought me a host of new readers, no doubt more of them middle-aged rather than young, though all three of these books went into paperback, not the cheapest sort because the illustrations had to be reproduced. And I seem to remember that all three of them were well received.

However, the one that gave me most pleasure to write was *The Edwardians*. There were various reasons why this should have been so. I shared my teens with this age, years that had a great formative influence upon me, as I have suggested more than once. Looking back on it, against the dark chaos of the First War (from which in some respects we never recovered), I saw it as a happy time, and so a pleasure to describe. Again, I felt it had been largely misunderstood. It was far from being all complacent conformism and *Land of Hope and Glory*. As well as the conformists it produced lively and engaging rebels, like Shaw and Wells and their admirers. It offered an unusually fine display of British genius in all the arts and the sciences. Its years were exceptionally fruitful. To describe all this was a labour of love. I confess I haven't re-read the book lately, but I can't help feeling that in it I captured most of what I felt. Whatever the verdict might be—if anybody is bothering about issuing one—I am left with the impression that it was the best of these three social histories, though I am certainly not ashamed of the other two.

The last of them, the Victorian one, came out in 1972. In this same year, I published something wildly different: *Over the Long High Wall: Some Reflections and Speculations on Life, Death and Time*. It came out to receive the kiss of death. I felt that even my publishers didn't want it, though they were too polite to tell me so. Nobody seemed to welcome it. I might have been bringing a skeleton out of a cupboard. Where it was not condemned, it met a hostile silence. I could have been advocating the murder of little children. I regard this book as the supreme flop of my career in publishing. Yet there was nothing wrong with it technically as a book; the writing was lively, never heavily boring; it covered the ground set out in its subtitle. But apparently it covered the wrong ground, said the wrong things. And what a change from the later 1930s, when the Time theories in my two chapters of autobiography had been favourably noticed, and my two 'Time Plays' had run successfully through a whole season! And I am not airing a personal grievance now: the argument goes far beyond that. The change was not in me but in the public, in the *zeitgeist*. It was as if passing-time and our inevitable extinction by it were now sacred topics, not to be challenged by old Priestley, still bumbling away.

A clever friend of mine, David Foster, author of *The Intelligent Universe*, came out of a long period dealing with advanced technology, with electronics and computers and the like, to take a look at our general culture. To my surprise—and I didn't know him then—he found in it what he boldly declared to be 'a death-wish'. Did this account for what happened to my *Long High Wall*? I have never questioned David Foster closely about this forthright judgment of his, which possibly goes too far, but it certainly didn't contradict my personal experience. Let us hazard a guess at what may have happened to the *Zeitgeist*.

Any speculation about Time, making it multi-dimensional, offers us a larger helping of life and experience. So does any suggestion that death does not extinguish us. But what if a great many people, once they have left their youth behind, don't welcome any enlargement of experience? What if they have had enough of this life, as they see it? They may dread the act of dying, yet in their heart of hearts they may look forward to this life being completely blotted out for ever and ever. No more experience, thank you, just an end of it! Such people might resent anything that disturbed this programme. They might be all the more eager to be rid of experience just because they had found it increasingly dull and boring—unlike the author of *Over the Long High Wall*. For their part, *they have had it*. And as far as this particular book is concerned, I have had it too. It is exactly the sort of book that ought to be in cheap paperback, then prominently displayed, so that younger people, not yet fixed in the death-wish, could relish it. It ought—it ought—but what a hope!

In my hurry to describe this disaster, I see I have overlooked a volume, already published in 1969. This is *Essays of Five Decades*, a generous selection of my essays covering half a century. My editor here, choosing the pieces with great skill, was Susan Cooper, a close and clever friend of ours, who wrote a whole book about me, calling it *A Portrait*. It pretends not to flatter me but of course it does, to my great satisfaction. Hurray for this —and also for choosing the essays, Susan! This substantial book went into paperback, though I never happen to see it around. They ought to have put a murdered blonde on the cover.

In 1973 I brought out *The English*, another illustrated book. It is a mixture of social analysis, opinion, and sketch portraits of major English characters; and though it can be read without pain

[39]

and with some profit, I am not enthusiastic about it—rather too much of a mixture. But some of the pictures offer you a treat.

We went to New Zealand and enjoyed everything so much in that beautiful country—only some of the people are beautiful but they are astonishingly friendly, perhaps because they are not all crowded together, as we are—that I felt I really had to write a book. So *A Visit to New Zealand* came out in 1974. They have some good painters out there, and I included some reproductions of their work, together with some attempts of my own in gouache. I don't know if the book did anybody much good here in England, but it pleased a lot of New Zealanders, who deserved some pleasure. I took a great fancy to that country, rather like a splendid kind of woman, at once beautiful and amiable. I think if I were a young man I might settle out there, if they'd have me. True, it is a long way from anywhere; but then that anywhere isn't what it used to be—too many people and too many of them disagreeable.

In that same year, 1974, came *Outcries and Asides*. Partly to explain it and partly to avoid praising myself, I shall quote some of the publishers' blurb on the inside of the jacket:

> This book, published in honour of the author's eightieth birthday, consists of more than two hundred short informal pieces—like so much 'Table Talk'—on a great variety of topics. . . Perceptive, stimulating, funny and profound, this is Priestley writing at the top of his bent.

And now for a little horror story. These last few months I have been amusing myself writing *Notes by the Way*, trying once again to be perceptive, stimulating etc. etc. Now I have just brought down, from the top of the house, where I keep the books I have written in a locked room, once a powder closet, a copy of *Outcries and Asides*. I haven't opened it since it came from the publishers. But now what have I found? Every other page or so shows me pieces that are twins to what I have recently been writing in *Notes by the Way*. In short, I have been innocently repeating myself, just like any daft old gaffer. About half these *Notes* could be—and will be, unless a fire is handy—chucked into the waste-paper basket. Well, I know what to do with them, but what may I have to start doing with myself? Funny still, perhaps; but no longer perceptive, stimulating, profound; just a forgetful repetitious old codger. Perhaps Jacquetta or Miss Pudduck (housekeeper) will have to hide my typewriter, and I will have to speak all further *Notes*, to attentive neighbours, on my way to and from the village shop.

After further dipping, and after recovering from the horror aspect, I find these *Outcries and Asides* both sensible and lively, even if not quite up to the blurb. Just as a tasting sample, here is a little piece on *Things*:

Among the imbecilities of our society is its attitude towards things. Never in the history of our species have more things been produced. Almost everything from the planet's future to a decent peace of mind is being sacrificed to more and more and more things things things. It is as if we were turning ourselves into a bigger sort of insect fixed into an idiotic pattern of manufacture and distribution. Yet at the same time we care less about things themselves than our grandfathers or forefathers did. Few of us really try to understand things, to take proper care of them, to cherish and love them. Once past childhood, which at least appreciates some things, increasingly we pay things less and less attention, seeing them as so much disposable stuff. If we are up-to-the-minute types, then we are already planning to rid ourselves of the boring wretched things we possess in order to welcome into the house whole vanloads of new bright things things things.

Am I flattering myself if I add that this piece says a good deal, enough for a longish article in the heavier newspapers, in very little space? The trouble with a Table Talk book like *Outcries and Asides* is that you cannot tell if you have brought it off or not. A large sale can't be expected; it doesn't attract lengthy reviews; and it doesn't encourage letters from readers, faced with such a variety of topics. But I enjoyed writing it, lost no money over it;

and at least had some lavish praise on the blurb. Moreover, I had reached eighty—about to live on borrowed time—when it appeared; and to this day haven't the least notion how many copies it sold. This is not the fault of William Heinemann Ltd: they are involved now with a dreamy and half-dotty octogenarian.

To write about painting, music, acting, clowning, all in one book seemed to me a wonderful idea. Eagerly I set to work on *Particular Pleasures*, 1975. And I was pleased with what I wrote. (And it had pictures too, lots of them.) The book hadn't been out more than a few weeks before I decided that I had been cheating myself with a rotten idea. The book was altogether too mixed, without a definite appeal in any one direction. It might be easy to read but it was hard to review. Instead of everybody wanting it, hardly anybody wanted it. Who was talking about *Particular Pleasures*? Nobody. But what about all these actors, actresses, comedians and clowns who appear in the book, their qualities nicely judged? I waited for their appreciative letters. I got exactly two, both from old friends, Peggy Ashcroft and Alec Guinness. Not a word from anybody else. No *Particular Pleasures* for them. (Perhaps they couldn't write; perhaps they couldn't even read; though now I must except Frankie Howerd, who was brought by Dulcie Gray to lunch with us, even as far as Alveston, Stratford-upon-Avon, and who proved to be a serious enquiring guest, no jokes at all.) Me and my *Particular Pleasures*! Next time I have a wonderful idea, I must take a longer and harder look at it. Oh—a few people told me or wrote that they had enjoyed the book—and I still felt that it had been a decent piece of work—but somebody ought to have warned me, before I had been too far involved, that I had been fooled by a bad idea.

The Carfitt Crisis: and two other stories, really two novellas and a short story, represented a serious experiment, not one I had ever tried before. *The Carfitt Crisis* and *The Pavilion of Masks* had existed for some years as plays. There was, I believe, nothing wrong with them as plays, but both had themes that I took—and still take—seriously, and I wanted to offer them to the public without the fuss and palaver of play production. But there was something else I wanted to do. This is best explained in the

Dedicatory Letter I wrote to my friend, Charles Pick, head of Heinemann:

> If any reader chooses to see these two novellas as an old writer's toys, I shan't take offence, even though the ideas that can be discovered in them are serious ideas important to us in the present age. The stories they tell were originally in dramatic form—though I have made many changes—and this has encouraged me to make an experiment in my manner of narration here, deliberately avoiding all but the barest description and refusing to offer the usual accounts, with which so many novels are over-loaded, of what my characters are thinking and feeling. This severely objective method, confining itself to what my characters say and do, may or may not be welcome, but at least it is a change. . . .

And this, I think, explains the experiment. I might add that in my not-so-humble opinion these two novellas would make superb television plays, but so far nobody has approached my agent to tell him so. And if both the BBC and ITV have a surfeit of good television plays, my viewing suggests they must be keeping them in a safe, somewhere.

But perhaps the themes of these two novellas are unacceptable. Let us take a quick look at them. *The Carfitt Crisis* is dominated by a strange man called Engram, who turns up to offer himself as unpaid cook and butler for the weekend. He is so highly conscious, so much aware of what is happening to the Carfitts and their guests (busy not understanding themselves) that he seems like a kind of magician. In *The Pavilion of Masks*, which has a romantic 1840s background, the Italian charlatan is really the hero. He deceives others but not himself, whereas the people he manipulates deceive themselves all the time, loudly proclaiming the opposite of what they are actually doing. (Like the great powers who say they want peace and prepare for war.) Though very different in background, story, style, there is a certain kinship between these novellas. In both of them, awareness, self-knowledge, mental honesty, are all important. And if this is not topical

[43]

and very much to the point, then I must be living in some other age. Meanwhile, what has been happening to *The Carfitt Crisis*? Roughly, I think, the answer is Not Much. But I enjoyed writing the book.

Found, Lost, Found—or The English Way of Life was another experiment, in style, manner, length, being only about 36,000 words. And why not? Unlike most writers, I like to bring out novels of various sizes. (*The Image Men*—my giant pet—is about 300,000 words.) No doubt I take advantage of my age and the fact that I have been with the same publisher—Heinemann—for half a century. I realize that a novelist uncertain of his publisher may want to keep to fairly standard length, somewhere between 60,000 and 80,000 words; but if I had my way there would be more quite short novels and more very long ones, depending of course on the tale to be told, the number of characters involved, the variety of settings. *Found, Lost, Found*, a cheeky work, would be intolerable if it ran to any length, whereas in 36,000 words I would be making a mere start with my Image experts. Has there been a sharp decline of interest in new fiction? If so, perhaps a movement away from a more or less standard length might help. Some novels could be sharpened and made more dramatic by being shortened. On the other hand, to risk a far larger scale, together with a rich variety of characters and settings, might return fiction to its Victorian importance. Bolder and more fruitful minds should be at work.

As I don't get press-cuttings and never ask my publisher to let me see any, I have no idea how this short cheeky novel was generally received. (And I don't propose to change my habits, not even to write this book.) I see only the reviews in the papers I regularly read. One chap was rather sour and decidedly unchivalrous, wanting, he said, to give my nice heroine, Kate Rapley, a kick in the pants. (A dangerous image for a reviewer, putting ideas into an author's head.) My Kate, after an earlier failure of a marriage, found herself immediately attracted to a man who obviously drank too much, and behaved like a sensible girl and not just another idiot. So she was dubious, a bit bossy, rather stubborn—no reviewer's girl-friend she—and at the same time enabled my hero and me to wander round England, with our eye on the sub-title of the novel, to which I recommend any new reader to pay attention. A feminine reviewer in the *Daily Telegraph* satisfied me. She began by saying that the allegory in this novel is obvious and thin, which surprised me because I didn't know any allegory was intended here; but then she continued, 'On another and more entertaining level'—really the only one I had in mind, dear—'it is a short, sweet, sunny book with some excellent comic scenes and a tender, happy ending.' An exact description, in my opinion. Perhaps only women— bless them!—should review short novels of mine. But some of the men were kind, and Philip Howard (a sharp critic of slovenly English himself) in the *Times* wrote: 'You do not have to agree with the tetchiness. And yet the darling...old buffer is still a beautiful writer...' Incidentally, my American publishers eagerly snapped up *Found, Lost, Found.*

I had had in mind for some time the idea of bringing out a biggish illustrated book on *English Humour.* This I did, beginning with Chaucer and finally arriving more or less at the present day. It is, I believe, an honest book. By that I mean that I included and praised authors and work that seemed to me genuinely comic, whether they were in fashion or out of it. This is tricky of course because personal taste in humour can be highly individual, and this means in effect that here honesty is really the best policy. (For example, I might have pleased a large body of readers by joining them in their chorus of praise for P. G. Wodehouse, but I preferred my own opinion to theirs.) Throughout I have taken the line that the true humorist is something more than a funny-man, having a sense of irony as well as of absurdity and in addition a fair measure of affection for his fellow creatures. So, for instance, two professional funny-men, the brothers Grossmith, suddenly transformed themselves into true humorists in their *Diary of a Nobody,* a little masterpiece. Moreover, my book has an important section, fully illustrated, on comic art. Can I hope —a trifle wistfully perhaps, because I am not in the schoolbook trade, highly remunerative and almost a closed shop—that this book might finally arrive in a number of schools? I am not thinking now about money, which I now collect for the benefit of the Inland Revenue and any crackpot ploys dreamt up by the government in power; but I like the idea of some young faces lighting up at some passages in my book. Incidentally, though writing it was agreeable enough, getting it ready with no help whatever (our secretary spending so much of her time with the monstrous imbecility of VAT) was a hard slog, bringing together all the works I needed, and then digging into them for the necessary quotations. It may surprise you to know, Prime Minister and Rt. Hon. Gents, that we authors earn our keep—and indeed rather more keep than you allow us.

Now I am in a muddle and a pickle, rather like those novelists who write a novel about a novelist writing a novel. For here among my books is this book, *Instead of the Trees*, which I am actually writing now, on this very page. How can I describe it when I am still working on it? But I might risk making one point. So far all the sections are shorter than they ought to be or than they would have been in my earlier 'chapters of autobiography'. There appears to be, in a writer of my age, a constant but curious abbreviating process, for ever cutting down instead of expanding. It is as if while seeing my own life being shortened I can't write at length on any subject. If this goes on, whatever *Instead of the Trees* may be, it will be no very substantial volume.

My very first book might be said to be without any substance. It was called *A Chapman of Rhymes*, was a collection of dubious verse, written in my teens before the First War and sent to be published, entirely at my own expense, during that war when I felt, foolishly, I ought to leave something behind. A little later, still alive and coming to my senses, I destroyed every copy I could lay hands on, now well aware of my folly. But only a month or two ago, a friend sent me a bookseller's catalogue in which this idiot publication was priced at something over £250. As an attempt at literature I would value it at well under 25p but of course there are such men as collectors, men of means quietly going out of their minds. No doubt if I had kept back a few copies, I might by this time have made what is often called a *nice thing* out of it. But I am doomed never to have an eye for a

[46]

nice thing, as I was reminded the other day, when I saw that a house I owned and then sold for £10,000 about sixteen years ago is now on the market at £145,000. I just have to go on earning my living, book after book.

But at least my second book, coming out while I was still up at Cambridge, wasn't published at my own expense. It was called *Brief Diversions* and was a cleverish mishmash of epigrams, parodies, fables. It had a curious history because, for some reason I have never understood, it attracted the favourable attention of the chief reviewers of the day. I imagined in my hopeful innocence, this would send people swarming to the bookshops, probably selling two or three thousand a week. But nothing of the sort happened, which might explain why I turned from optimism to pessimism, where I have remained, shrugging away, ever since. True, I had an explosive 'bestseller' in *The Good Companions*. But what happened then? I was blamed by the fastidious minority for writing it at all. I was blamed then for years by the disappointed majority for not writing the same kind of novel but offering it novels quite different. No, of course you can't win, as people say, but you can do the next best thing—and that is to forget your readership and write what you dam' well want to write, for after all *you* have to spend most time with whatever it is. And that is what I am doing, here and now, with something called *Instead of the Trees*.

VI

It is important to understand, because of what follows, that I am not a hero. I am fairly average—half brave, half a coward—perhaps rather more apprehensive because I am an imaginative man. Now it happens I have been in situations of great danger, chiefly of course in the First War, in which I was a casualty three times; but also, to a lesser extent, in the Second War, dodging about in blitzes on my way to and from broadcasting. And on a few rare occasions in peace time, when, for example, in a plane temporarily out of control when I was also injured. I must emphasize the great danger—not for glory; I have none to claim —but all the better to explain exactly what happened during these moments. I must add here that I am sure my experience was not unique, though oddly enough no similar experiences have ever been described to me, though I can't help feeling they must be in print somewhere.

This is what occurred, not once but many times. It looked as if I might be blown to pieces or (in the plane) fried alive. But just when terror was at its height—or, better, its sick depth—all was changed and what was happening didn't matter. Some part of me—or somebody who wasn't me—took over. Whatever took over wasn't frightened, not panic-stricken at all, and that dreadful shrinking, that curdling in the stomach, completely vanished. What took their place was a mild curiosity. Well, well—this is what it's going to be like, being blown to pieces or fried alive in a plane, as if it were just another curious experience, to add to hundreds of others. I might have been turned into my own biographer. And if this had happened only once, I wouldn't be writing about it. But it probably happened at least a score of times, and always the same odd experience.

Ten to one there is a school of thought ready to declare, without much hesitation, that a psychological mechanism intervened to free me from dread and the urge to panic. Now this is all very well—and mechanisms have long been in fashion—but certain questions suggest themselves. Who or what put the mechanism to work? It couldn't be the ego, fully engaged in trying to face the terror, unable to think in terms of elaborate psychological rescue arrangements. Again, there is this sense of being suddenly taken over by somebody or something quite different, with mild curiosity taking the place of terror. Unless we are victims of dissociation—meat and drink for alienists—we have only one ego, not two. And clearly one ego can't take over itself so dramatically. So we have to look outside the ego.

Now the immediate effect—and I am describing a score of occasions—was as follows. Because of this new attitude of mind, which certainly hadn't been mine a few moments before—cool curiosity replacing terror—I felt I had been taken over by an Immortal Observer. But do I believe that I am carrying round with me, ready for these crises, any such Immortal Observer? I do not. Nor, being an agnostic, do I believe that saints or angels, in their compassion, might intervene. (Often I wish I did.) What then are we left with? The ego can't rescue itself, and there is this definite sense of being taken over by something superior to the ego. But I won't accept—though with some reluctance—anything like an Immortal Observer. What then do I accept? It is the temporary emergence of the Self, taking over the ego.

This could be the Self as described by Jung, the conclusion and crown of his process of individuation. To this I shall return later. Here I must say something about Jung himself, who has had a very considerable influence on my thought for the last forty years or so. Not as a patient but as an admirer I had several long talks with him, and we exchanged a number of letters. Now I am a rather sceptical fellow, with a very small bump of reverence, but this seemed to me a great man. He was large physically and even larger mentally. He could be very easy and convivial, with many a laugh over a pipe and a drink, and yet remain formidable in essence, a deep wise old bird, half a chum and half a magician. The sweep and depth of his scholarship, his knowledge, sheer experience, were astounding. I have met a fair number of psychologists who seemed to me the worst possible advertisements of their particular systems. Jung was the opposite. If I had been a neurotic patient I would have felt better after half-an-hour of him. Incidentally, he never encouraged creative writers or artists of any kind to consult him, because he believed that creative work provided its own constant therapy. We people attended to ourselves as we went along.

What follows here is not addressed to Jungians. It is meant to catch the attention of those who really know nothing about him and what he discovered and worked upon, people who may have been misled by silly references to him and his work by journalists who hadn't a clue. And—first—a useful tip. Don't go at once directly to Jung himself. Try the books—and there are several very good ones—all written by his assistants or more experienced followers, who explain in a fairly systematic fashion the scope and character of Jung's work. (By the way, most of the terms from depth psychology that have found their way into our ordinary talk—as for example *complex*, *introvert*, *extravert*—come from Jung.) But why do this, ignoring at first the old master himself? There are two reasons. A ground-plan of what is a complicated system is very useful in itself. Secondly, Jung's own books and printed lectures—and there are some admirable translations—come out of a full and indeed overflowing mind, with reference following reference, example piled on example, excursions into distant lands or remote mythologies, explorations deep into the dark unconscious, so that the total effect can at first be bewildering. Afterwards, with the ground-plan still in mind, Jung's own works can offer an exhilarating experience. If a big tasting sample is wanted, then try *C. G. Jung: Psychological Reflections, Edited by Jolande Jacobi*. Also, strongly recommended, are Jung's own *Memories, Dreams, Reflections*, recorded and edited by Aniela Jaffé; and the large illustrated volume, *Man and his Symbols*, conceived by Jung in his last days.

What I, never a neurotic patient, owe first of all to Jung is his all-important idea of the unconscious, not simply the personal unconscious (the *Id* of Freud) but also the collective unconscious, going down to a great depth of human experience. His unconscious is as much part of ourselves as our consciousness; and indeed to a creative writer at times a far more important part of ourselves. For what happens when we are working at our highest pitch? A play or a novel seems to be arriving magically, without any conscious effort. It is coming, as dreams come, from the unconscious. Out of our experience and technique, we may give what is communicated a shape—with consciousness working at an unusually high speed—but the essential creativity is coming from the unconscious. It supplies the genie of the magic lamp and ring.

The Jungian unconscious tends to act also as a kind of balance-wheel. If we are too one-sided in our conscious life, the unconscious stresses the neglected other side. So a man overtly ambitious and determined to be successful at all costs may have very disturbing dreams, may find himself haunted by dark premonitions and vague feelings of impending disaster, all of which may result in his becoming neurotic, incapable of continuing his dazzling career. The unconscious is warning him that he is hopelessly one-sided. And Jung said over and over again that modern society, ignoring what is coming from the unconscious and being desperately one-sided, has encouraged one kind of disaster after another, as we know all too well. We may not be as complacent as we were, but our overcrowded mental hospitals don't suggest we have achieved a healthy balance between consciousness and the unconscious.

It is this balance that has been achieved by this Self of Jung's brought about by the process of individuation. Expressing what has happened in spatial terms, we can say that this Self has moved away from the ego to be closer to the boundary between consciousness and unconscious. Or we can say that now it is constantly aware of what is being prompted by the unconscious. This returns me to my moments of great danger, during which I might appear to be taken over by an Immortal Observer. The latter might be the Self of Jung's, dominating the ego and reporting what comes from the unconscious. But why Immortal? Because the collective unconscious contains elements that are ancient indeed, possibly covering a vast time span that can seem like immortality to us. And the calm curiosity can arrive from a breadth and depth of experience hard for us to imagine. Dismissing the Immortal Observer, I do at least offer a Jungian explanation of what might happen on these desperate occasions.

I will make a further though less certain attempt. It will be in terms of the system taught by Gurdjieff and Ouspensky, which has not been without influence on my beliefs. I never knew either of them, but I was acquainted with several of their more prominent disciples, such as Orage, J. G. Bennett, Kenneth Walker, and have read all around Gurdjieff and Ouspensky. As there used to be many silly allusions to these men and their 'groups', I must add that most of their followers were far from being misty crackpots and sentimental dreamers but highly-educated professional men and women. And indeed what they were taught was not easy and soft. It asked for severe mental discipline. Men were 'asleep' or 'machines' unless they heightened and sharpened consciousness, becoming more closely aware of what went on in their minds. One of their exercises was 'remembering oneself', not losing oneself in objectivity but being constantly aware of one's own personality in various situations. Another was dividing attention between what was being observed and the self that was observing. Most men, the teaching went, had no consistent enduring 'I', which was what had to be achieved, but were under the influence of one different 'I' after another, as if in their inner life there was a microphone that was seized by one different man after another, as if instead of one integrated person there was a repertory company hard at work. One of their disciplines I can strongly recommend to all readers because I have followed it myself. This is to resist the invasion of the mind by what was known as 'negative emotions'—blinding anger, envy, jealousy, malice, or even constant worry—because not only did these have a bad effect on character but they were also appalling wasters of energy that could be used for better purposes. This is entirely true, as I know from personal experience. If I have been energetic in my professional life, it is partly because I have largely kept these negative emotions at bay.

The system was based on an elaborate cosmic theory and might dally with recurrence and some undying Circle of Conscious Humanity; but we don't have to consider them here. What concerns us is its insistence upon an enduring consistent personality, a central Self not for ever chopping and changing, a steady heightened and sharpened consciousness. This returns me to my moments of great danger and the taking over of the terrified ego by my Immortal Observer. Just as there might have been a sudden emergence of Jung's individuated Self, so too, from some study of this system, however casual and unsystematic this might have been, isn't it just possible that at these desperate times, without any willing on my part, my ego was taken over by the kind of Self the system was telling us to achieve? Do I owe my sudden deliverance not to any Immortal Observer, hard to justify, but simply to some rather desultory reading in Jung or this Gurdjieff–Ouspensky system? If so, then I can consider myself a lucky man. For certainly I was deeply afraid—I repeat, I am no hero—and then I was no longer afraid but just calmly curious. I reject, as I have already declared, the mere psychological mechanism, for what part of me could have set it in motion. More reluctantly, I must also reject the Immortal Observer theory. So what has been left, to pop up, to take over, to rescue me? Nothing but a constant curiosity and a fair amount of close reading, bringing about the sudden emergence of one or other of these superior Selves. Is this good enough? I don't know. What I do know is that time after time I have been horribly frightened and then, a magical stroke, terror has vanished and a calm curiosity has taken its place. Yes indeed—time after time—and I have described what has happened with all the honesty at my command. True, none of these events is recent, and now I am tottering into old age, trying to avoid anything like a very dangerous situation. Even so, later this very year, a doctor concluding a thorough examination might look me hard in the eye and tell me there is something very serious I ought to know. Will one of these superior Selves take me over and rescue me again? I can only hope so.

VII

I must have been close to sixty when I started painting, not having done any since I left school, a world away. What set me off I cannot remember now. I don't believe I had had it in mind for some time before: it must have been an odd sudden impulse. Had I been living in London then, I might have gone in search of some instruction, because I didn't imagine for a moment that I didn't need any. But I was living in the Isle of Wight, and I was working hard, so I decided I would try to learn something as I went along. What I was after was a hobby that would engage me when we were away on holiday. We were still travelling widely—and indeed continued to do so for some years—and I think I wanted to respond, in a modestly creative fashion, to the challenge of new strange landscapes. I doubt if a real artist in painting, unless he happens to feel rather stale, thinks in such terms: he sets to work on whatever catches and holds his eye, enabling him to produce his own personal vision of this world. I didn't even tell myself I was that sort of man. I could only hope to be a bumbling old amateur dauber, amusing myself.

Even so, I hoped not to be wretchedly shockingly bad, making my wife and friends wince and turn away in embarrassment. This was not unreasonable. After all, I had known many real artists; I had been looking at pictures for years and years; I had bought any number of them, and there were masters on my walls; and though untaught and blundering and beginning far too late, I felt I might have a go without making a complete ass of myself. Resisting the temptation to dash out and capture the downs and cliffs of the Isle of Wight, I stayed at home to try to relate eye and brush, really beginning very sensibly indeed. (Other beginners, please note.) Buying oil paints and boards, I set up the usual elementary still-life assemblies of bottles, cigar boxes, and the like, gradually bringing in bowls and fruit. I seem to have kept a few of these early attempts here in the little painting room (unused now) at Kissing Tree House, Alveston, and though they are no creations of wonder and joy, they are really not too bad, and certainly served their turn, bringing eye and brush together, not entirely without tone.

But why didn't I go on from oils to watercolour, the queen of English media? Wasn't I brought up among the watercolourists who explored the Yorkshire dales? Can't I show in the drawing-room here works by Frances Towne, Girtin, Cotman, Varley, with lesser watercolours all over the house? Yes, I can, and that is the trouble. Men of sixty can't begin to master the art of water-colour. Any fool of course can paint a bad watercolour—the country is be-daubed with them—but a watercolour worth show-ing to anybody demands a mastery of the difficult little art. You can't mess about with it. You must know exactly what you are doing and how to do it. Even with goodish men, who earn their living this way, it tends to be hit-or-miss, as I know from going through many portfolios. Even the masters must have had, un-known to us, many failures. I failed from the start, and though I have tried again on occasion, dreaming of some sudden miracu-lous gift descending on me, I have never been any good with this favourite medium.

So watercolours were out. But so too were oils. This was be-cause I wanted to do my painting on holiday, usually far from home, and oils in these circumstances were too heavy, clumsy and messy, at least for an amateur, not clever and experienced with equipment. So I decided to compromise and settle for gouaches, which—for the uninitiated—are opaque watercolours, generally demanding tinted paper, not the white paper that must be cunningly used as a highlight by the watercolourist. Now while it is true that masters have occasionally tried gouaches, often for quick bright sketches, the real art of landscape painting belongs either to oils or watercolours, and I announce myself here as a rather low fellow, with no pretensions to mastery. But then I was only amusing myself while on holiday. I wasn't aiming at exhibitions, press cuttings, sales. What I wanted to do—to

[55]

quote Charles the Wrestler—was to fleet the time carelessly as they did in the golden world. And this is what I have done, and nobody can say I haven't.

However, most of the actual painting I had to do in a hurry. We were usually on the way to somewhere and so couldn't stop too long. Not that it worried me that I couldn't linger and take more trouble, if only because I probably didn't know what trouble to take. Moreover, it is a fact that most of my better pictures had been done in half-an-hour or so. But what happiness came from the concentration, the deep absorption, and the result if I felt I had caught something essential and (to me) memorable in the landscape! Of course I might have described it in writing, returning to my trade, but there was an instant magic in handling brushes and paints, matching or contrasting colours, bringing character into design, attempting an over-all tone. No wonder— at least in my experience—painters are happier persons than writers.

It is true of course that I had a professional responsibility in writing whereas I could just amuse myself freely in painting. Even so, I was never simply larking about. Though no doubt a blundering elderly amateur, dashing away with my gouaches, I was trying in my own fashion to repay a debt I owed to the landscapes in question, many of them far removed from anything I had known at home. Probably I was situated somewhere between a genuine professional painter and a tourist busy taking colour photographs of a scene that attracted him. At the worst, my gouaches—and I have scores of them—revive some of our pleasantest memories, and do it better than photographs can do. Most of them are down in the cellar, quite securely housed, but I keep some favourites in my bedroom. A brief list will show how wide-ranging they are, these landscapes: Lake Sevan in Soviet Armenia; mountain country in County Mayo; moorland in Central Wales; a glimpse of the New England coast; another of Morocco; another of Ceylon; Death Valley in California; a Yorkshire dale; and two from Guatemala, very good painting country. And so it would go on, down in the cellar, which occasionally supplies me with others to hang or a present or two to family and close friends. A few of them have been noticed amiably, not with sudden joy but not with disgust neither, by one of our greatest artists and also by our most fastidious critic of the visual arts—*there*!

Painting these gouache landscapes has brought me a great deal of pleasure—and indeed perhaps something a little deeper, a creative response to another kind of country. They have brought me no fame, no public applause, for I have never asked for any and know I don't deserve any. But a little applause in private, with some gratifying hanging on family walls. And of course all that happy absorption round the world—I have painted on every continent except Antarctica—together with a wonderful excuse to cut short mere sight-seeing, which I detest after an hour or so. The cost? (Of the painting, I mean; not the travel.) So modest that I could probably go out next week and sell three or four pictures that would more than cover the total outlay. What money couldn't buy are all those happy hours when I sat down, opened my fat brown-canvas painting bag, stared hard for a few minutes and then set to work, forgetting everything else.

But am I trying to sell something here? Yes, I am. Not my pictures nor anybody else's—but an idea. While it is true that painting as a hobby is now fairly widespread in this country, I think it could be spread wider. To begin with, there are all the people who have said to me, 'I don't see how you've done it, not at your age. I wouldn't even know how to start.' To which I've replied, time after time, 'But how do you know if you've never *tried*.' We don't know what we can do until we try. Why not have a go? You're still younger than I was when I began.' (I say that to women whatever their age.) For all I know—and they know—in a year or so they might be creating delicious water-colours, well beyond my capacity, restricted to lumpy gouaches. All except my skies, my best feature, better than those of many professionals. I never do the clouds with a brush but always, working fast, with my fingers. And there now—that might give somebody a start, and I won't have written this section in vain.

VIII

I suspect that my idea of happiness differs from that of most people. It is because of this that I have often been at cross-purposes with them. My happiness is well removed from pleasure. It is not simply enjoyment. Though never slow with a grumble, I have been all my life a great enjoyer, ranging from Beethoven's *Missa Solemnis* to any fine large pork pie with a darkish crust. (And didn't I write a book called *Delight*?) I am no finicky taster of life but have always brought with me a splendid appetite. If praise is deserved at all, I pour it out with never a hint of a growl. For many years I reviewed books of my own choosing; then if I disliked a book, could find nothing good to say of it, I never gave it a notice; I would praise or keep silent. But all this enjoyment, to my mind, has no connection with happiness. Neither has a contented busyness, which many people remember as giving them a happy time. I am not against this judgment, which seems to me reasonable enough, but it is not for me.

My happiness has a special quality, not to be found any morning, evening, lazy afternoon. I am not now mistaking it for ecstasy, much rarer still. But my happiness can't be planned for, arranged, built up. It suddenly arrives out of the blue where it really belongs. There is no *excuse* for it. It is rather as if a fantastic bird had alighted near me and then burst into song. Or as if I walked down a familiar road and found myself inside a great blue bubble. Very soon, no doubt, the bird will fly away or the bubble will dissolve into a few scattered drops. I am never given fat helpings of my happiness. I can't call with it at the bank or take it to dine out at a neighbour's. Forty-nine times out of fifty I am alone when it happens, perhaps out walking or having a bath. But suddenly—there it is—and I realize that I am happy. (I agree there can be a retrospective sense of happiness—and some people

[58]

would argue there is no other kind—but clearly here I am at odds with such people, my experience always being immediate and quite definite.) Such then is my happiness.

Now let us turn over the coin so that its bright face is hidden. The dull side is seen on those occasions when I have been expected to be happy, when people have said, 'You must be feeling very happy.' And there is no sign of this. My face—heavy enough, anyhow—announces that my spirits, if anything, have been drooping. There I am—refusing to feel happy. What is the matter with me? I must be a miserably ungrateful or arrogant fellow, with utterly unreasonable expectations. Who am I—to shrug or scowl when any decent man would be beaming? This is the last time we bother with this chap. Why waste our praises and applause on him? We'll keep them for a more modest friendly man. And that, madam, is how I give myself a bad name.

Yet I am really innocent. Indeed, there is an almost childlike innocence in my idea of happiness, always coming unexpectedly out of the blue. Remember, I make no claim on it. If it descends upon me, well and good and even better. But this *You must be feeling very happy* stuff really belongs to another world, one of accounts, of debits and credits, of getting on in this life, of creeping up to the Top (whatever that is); all a long way from that fantastic bird that suddenly alights and sings, from that blue bubble you enter on a walk or in the bath. And all this is not what is understood by a whole series of bystanders. I have already declared in print that while I have a lot of talent, I have no genius. And I was wrong. I have a genius for being misunderstood. For instance, about happiness.

IX

Can any man ever escape the influences of his boyhood and youth? Certainly not, I believe, if he is a writer. I have been thinking about my own boyhood and youth and trying to determine what effect they may have had on my own work. This took me back to a suburb of Bradford in the years before the First War. A point that must be made at once is that living was very cheap then, so that continuous hospitality didn't really cost very much. (Whisky, for example, was three-and-sixpence a bottle, and a box of fifty cigars, quite good enough for guests, could be had for under a pound. It is worth remembering that male conviviality has been more and more savagely taxed.) Now my parents had many friends and were warmly hospitable. Apart from close friends, who were always 'popping in' (as they said then), my parents had a whole circle of friends, neighbours, friendly acquaintances, who came to parties at our house, sometimes to compete in whist drives. Then they had four tables set out after a vast high tea, which I tucked into after the guests had gone into the next room to start their whist; and at other times simply to enjoy a jolly evening with music. They went out a lot themselves, of course, but there I didn't follow them, being too young most of that time, and my memory clings to what happened in our house.

During the Christmas and New Year season, which lasted two or three weeks, there were parties galore and then I went out, to close friends of the family, as often as I stayed in; though by the time I reached youth from boyhood I had my own circle of hospitable friends and certain open houses where I knew I could have a good time. I was in demand partly because I could play the piano and accompany the various singers, from the women who sang *A May Morning* and Tosti's *Goodbye* to the bassaritones, not always hitting the right note, who asked us to beware because *Many brave hearts are asleep in the deep*. But I was also in demand because I could recite humorous monologues and was a lively performer in charades. (You might say I *showed off*, something I have been doing ever since, in one way or nother.) But on Christmas Day and a few similar occasions (including funerals) there were parties of a very different sort. This was when remote elderly relatives solemnly descended upon us, as strange to me in boyhood as dinosaurs. There would be great-aunts, all with loose false teeth, who spoke in broad dialect, hard to understand anyhow, of relatives even more remote that I could never remember meeting at any time—creatures out of mythology. And indeed, on all these occasions, I sat trying to listen or handing out slices of pound cake, never at ease because I seemed to be on the edge of another world.

Trying to capture the whole scene—after at least sixty-five years—I find myself entertaining a confused but rich blur of hospitality and conviviality, of gossip and jokes and political argument, of roast pork and sherry trifle, of cigar smoke and whisky toddy, of upholstered ladies and red-faced loud-voiced husbands beginning to sweat a little, most of whom, at the time, seemed to me not quite real people but so many comic characters unconsciously performing for my benefit. All of it—from the 'popping in' with the rapidly improvised supper of potted-meat sandwiches and cold apple pie, to the sumptuous high teas and crowded parties—was taking place in an atmosphere that I took for granted then and felt would go on for ever. And it didn't. After I came back from the First War, it was thinner and colder and it stayed that way. The food shortages, the constant anxiety, the black casualty lists, had all played their part. But something else had happened to which it is impossible to give an exact name; it might be roughly described as a loss of innocence, of trust in this world, this life. In the part of the country I knew best, there was a drop in the social temperature. The old easy and warm hospitality of my boyhood and youth was hard to find.

Now we return to this question of influences. Is some of my work haunted by a certain feeling of nostalgia? Does it suggest

we have lost something along the way? Very well—the answer is
Yes. What, then, is the matter with me? Some people, quite close
to me, are ready with a reply to that. In their opinion I am simply
lamenting my vanished boyhood and youth. My enemy is time.
Other people, not close to me, would provide a different answer.
They would say I am a sentimentalist, and so take every chance
of behaving like one, mooning away and unwilling to face facts.
But I disagree sharply with both these sets of opinions. Let us
take each one in turn. I declare emphatically that I don't miss my
boyhood and youth, for I am not a fool and I know very well
they had to vanish. No, what I do miss, just enough to feel a
certain melancholy, is what accompanied my boyhood and youth,
what happened then in a particular atmosphere, even in a world
that changed, becoming harder and colder.

Again, the charge of sentimentality just won't do. To rebut it
will ask a brutal question and then answer it directly. Taken as a
whole were the people of—let us say—1912 better than people as
they are today? And I say they were. There can be regress as well
as progress, and it is a kind of sentimentality to deny this. The
whole scene is darker now than it was then. True, a monstrous
and quite unnecessary war was on its way then. But, for all we
know, another war, final and fatal, may be on its way now, and
even if it should be averted the total scene is far darker, with its
mounting crime, vandalism, terrorism, insane violence. People
then were free from strains and stresses that now keep mental
hospitals over-crowded. They were not so hard, not so cold, not
so self-seeking; they could contrive to be easy-going and warmly
hospitable, as I have already shown.

However, I will make one admission. As I have also already
shown, there was about those days—and nights—a certain cosiness, far less obvious today. Now cosiness of this kind has a particular appeal to women, who love to feel that people they are fond
of are under one roof. Very well, but I am not a woman. No, but
I am essentially a creative type of man, and in every man of my
sort there is a feminine element, urging us towards creation just
as most normal women long to have a baby. And so far as modern
living has moved away from cosiness, so this feminine element in

[62]

s feels dissatisfied and might wish to return to other times, other
fe-styles. And I suggest that all this is happening on a deeper
evel than sentimentality reaches. I also suggest that I have kept
a sharp eye on the social scene throughout my professional career,
nd that eye has been rarely misted by vague sentimental long-
ngs.

It is an eye—and now I return to influences from boyhood and
outh—that has always been ready to observe and record comic
haracters. As we have already seen, I must have known a pro-
ession of them from my earlier experiences, during which we
annot help seeing older people as comic appearances, sometimes
uge and daft enough—to us at that age—to seem like creatures
ut of mythology. So what has happened to me when at work?
ime after time, writing long novels, I have peopled the scene
vith scores and scores of minor comic characters, not because I
vanted to imitate Dickens—I have never wanted to imitate any-
ody; I am my own man—but because I was driven to it by
ecollections of my own boyhood and youth. Not that I was ever
ttempting portraits—that is a bad way of going about it,
veakening creation—but I was returning to the social atmosphere
f my boyhood and youth, trying to land new strange fish out of
he same kind of teeming waters. I was, in a sense, returning to
ny younger self, not seeing people as entirely real—and so prob-
bly tragic—but in the sharp bright light of youthful caricature.
may have overdone it—a fault of mine—but at least out of that
ld yeasty mash I have fetched enough minor comic characters to
ill a daft suburb or a semi-lunatic village. Some readers have told
ne they 'fell about laughing'. A few have announced that they
ould barely raise a smile. They must have had a very different
oyhood and youth—if any.

[63]

X

My first landing in New York took place in February 1931, from the old *Olympic*, a friendly ship for all her creaking and groaning (A first-class passage, with a large cabin all to yourself and with it every luxury, then cost £45.) For the benefit of some of my contemporaries, who also kept crossing the Atlantic, I might call a brief halt here, to remember those liners. They had to be ships and first-class hotels at one and the same time, a tricky business. They had personality too, so that seasoned travellers had definite preferences. My own favourite was not the *Olympic* but the *Aquitania*, somehow the best all-round ship. I cared nothing for the *Majestic* and the *Berengaria* and I never took to the two *Queens*, the *Mary* and the *Elizabeth*, which had enormous public rooms but smaller cabins than the older liners. (Going the way that hotels have gone.) Being a good sailor I always enjoyed these voyages to New York, always finding somebody I was glad to meet. During a particularly rough eastward passage, when there was hardly anybody about, I spent a lot of time with John Buchan, making friends at once: he was a more open-minded man than his popular tales suggested.

However, there was one snag towards the very end of these westward voyages. Before you were able to land in New York though within sight of its enfabled towers, a gang of newspaper men came aboard, pencils and copypaper at the ready. These were the notorious 'ships reporters', so many brazen pests whom later I learnt to dodge. But on this, my first arrival, in all innocence I gave them what they seemed to want, a load of cheerful nonsense. Gleefully they set down every word, and no doubt added some imbecilities of their own. It would have been better for me if I had leapt into the middle of them, my fists whirling For this nonsense—together with their own—I paid a very heavy price, not only then but for years afterwards, when indeed—to keep the game going when I had stopped playing it—*whole interviews were invented and attributed to me*. I was not just another goddam British author coming over to grab some dollars, I was also *anti-American*—yes, sir! This baleful legend lingered on for years and years, and I am not sure I am entirely free from it even now. With the result that though I like America (though not its Press) and have visited it over and over again, at my own expense and not with an eye on anybody's dollars, I don't believe America has ever liked me.

Of course this statement has to be qualified. A number of individual Americans—and there are some close friends among these —have liked me very much. I still get some heart-warming letters from American readers. But the people at large ceased to take an interest years ago, ever since the early successes of *The Good Companions* and *Angel Pavement* and of my first play in New York, *Dangerous Corner*. Perhaps this is my own fault. Was I a better man then? No, I was not. I have published other novels, at least as good as those two. I have had more important plays produced, some of them all over the world. Not one has been really successful in New York. And most of the books have had dim silly little reviews. (I never have press-cuttings but my American publishers have an unfortunate habit, discouraged by me, of sending copies of reviews.) Once I declared in print that I tended to be a highbrow to lowbrows and a lowbrow to highbrows. This has done me little or no harm here in England or in Europe, but I fancy it has played the devil with me in America, where highbrowism and lowbrowism are taken very seriously indeed.

There are some little ironies here. Not only do I like America— defying that old legend—but I have actually seen a great deal more of it than almost all my American friends, visiting Iowa City or Tombstone, Arizona, when they were staying in Paris or Venice. I have in my time been fascinated by—even falling in love with—the sheer size and bewildering variety of the United States. (Though a ruthlessly standardized culture has increasingly diminished this variety in its social aspect.) A combination of lecture tours and travel notes for books and articles must have taken me, at one time or another, to about half the states in the Union, to scores and scores of cities and towns my American friends have never visited at all. And in most of those places I have encountered the same warmth and instant generosity so characteristic of the American people. And here I will add at once that the world, so easily delivered over to envy, has long been less than grateful and fair to the generosity and fellow-feeling of America itself. There are people in this world, for ever sneering at America, who have never spent half-an-hour wondering how they could help persons less fortunate than themselves. And I couldn't exclude a lot of my countrymen from this base category.

We English can't show the same kindness and immediate hospitality but we are better in at least one respect: we don't take offence so hastily, perhaps because we feel rather more secure inside ourselves. True, I am not a very tactful fellow—especially when I am feeling tired—but it is only in the Middle West I have been able to offend whole towns, an impossible feat, I think, anywhere in Europe. I have been made to feel, while hastily packing, that if I stayed another couple of days I might be lynched. Moreover, certain individual Americans have behaved in a most mysterious fashion. I am not referring now to friends, all staunch over the years, but to people who were the friendliest acquaintances when we entertained them in London but then later, in New York, would be quite distant, even hostile, as if I had been saying dreadful things about them, when in fact I had been doing nothing of the kind, my feelings not having changed at all. I may be wrong about this—having had a fairly wide cosmopolitan circle of acquaintances—but it is only with certain Americans that I remember this happening. They never seem more suspicious than other people—rather less so, I fancy—yet their feelings can change in this sudden unaccountable fashion. Does New York do something to them?

It has always done something to me. During my early visits it excited me and (secretly) overawed me. This was before I had recourse to sleeping pills, so that I always felt short of sleep when I was there, and often suspected that nearly everybody else needed more sleep too. The buildings were too large, the city too rich, with the spoils of whole continents being offered for sale along Fifth Avenue. It was all terribly exciting until, with familiarity, I began to wonder what all the excitement was about. When boredom crept in, there was irritation too, because all the New Yorkers I met seemed to be crazy about the same thing—the same book, the same play, the same restaurant or night club, the same parlour tricks. There was a kind of herd instinct at work in those canyons between the ridiculously tall buildings, in a city erected for giants but largely inhabited by crazy dwarfs. Am I being unfair? Of course I am, but then this was never 'my town', much lower in my esteem than San Francisco and New Orleans or even, I think, Chicago, which had at least a brutal strength of its own. I never really like hotels anywhere, but I think I disliked New York hotels more than any. They seemed to be staffed by cynical refugees from Central Europe at the reception desks, ancient Irishwomen to do the rooms, and the sweepings of anthropological institutes pretending to be waiters in the dining-rooms. And again, for any visitor not a tycoon, it is not a friendly city, tending to be cynical and sour; or at least that's how it seemed when I was there last.

As soon as you move west or south from the city, everybody tells you that New York isn't America. But I think that in many respects it is. New York decides what is *in* and what is *out*. (I write here as an old *out*.) It decides what books should be read, what plays should be seen, what art (however silly) should be bought. And if, as a writer from overseas, you have never felt comfortable and at home in New York, suspecting its judgment in that over-charged atmosphere, then you are going to be out of luck with a large section of the American public. You are liable to be at the mercy of a certain type of New York critic—and I have one in mind—whose work uses as fuel a horrid mixture of swagger and bile. As a dramatist a good part of my income still arrives from productions abroad, all over the world, of plays I wrote 30 to 40 years ago. But not from New York, never from New York. And now it is a pleasure to forget that city and to think about the other America I have known so well.

[67]

I have spent many happy days in various parts of New England, especially in the crisp and multi-coloured fall. But what chiefly returns to memory, warmed by enduring affection, is the South-West, which I have explored from Death Valley in California to Rainbow Bridge in Utah. For Arizona, which I know best, I can actually feel a kind of homesickness, almost as if I had lived there, an Indian wandering in the desert, in some other ancient existence. I have travelled far and wide, all over and round the world, but no other distant countryside gives me that particular feeling. I went there again, a few years ago, finding it completely unchanged away from the main roads. But this can hardly be repeated, not with direct taxation in Britain as high as 83%, a murderous imposition.

What I feel I would miss now if I returned would be those wonderful long-distance trains of the 1930s, when, early one morning, you would look out of the window and see the magic desert, still not in full sunlight, rolling by towards your other home. And again, the rough-and-ready but satisfying hospitality (very cheap too) of the roadside motor camps still not transformed expensively into motels, part of a newer and more demanding world. Moreover, there were still *characters* in that South-West I knew, ranchers and cowboys and those failed business men, all lean and leathery, who came down from the hills where they had been 'dry-washing' for gold and earning just enough to buy more beans and bacon. This was, I suppose, a last glimpse of pioneering America, and one we hear or read so little about, so far away from Madison Avenue or Wall Street, and one capable of attracting and holding a man's affection. Sometimes, here in my study, I take a drink of Old Time Charcoal Mellowed Tennessee Whiskey and then there rises from the glass, out of an aroma very different from that of my familiar Scotch, a whole lost continent, rings of friendly faces, echoes of lively talk, and that strange melancholy sound made by trains in the night, following the old Santa Fé trail. Yes, sir, I like America, whatever America thinks about me.

XI

If I had to describe myself very briefly—and waving away modesty and gentlemanly understatement—I think I would say that I am a life-enhancing pessimist. Let us take the pessimism first. A man would be out of his mind if he called upon me to show him 'the bright side'. Both sides are dark in my view and probably will soon be darker. Clouds—which incidentally I paint with some skill—wear no silver linings for me. Today is bad— and tomorrow will be worse. If you ask for a broader aspect, then I will tell you that civilization has been on the decline since about 1912. (For example, torture has come back.) Would I like to go back to 1912? Certainly, without hesitation; though no doubt if I was back there I would start grumbling. There are some decent quiet pessimists, who perhaps merely lift an eyebrow; but I am not one of them. I am ready to complain not only about what is happening to me but also about the whole human race, with its persistent stupidity, folly and cruelty.

Any notion of progress seems to me idiotic. We go from bad to worse. I am now living in a half-ruined country, which imposes the severest taxes in the world, thanks to a succession of blunders for which, at an earlier and more sensible time, ministers might have been impeached. An optimist in the contemporary world is drifting towards lunacy, and may soon be announcing that he is Napoleon or an egg. How any thoughtful man can escape pessimism, I can't imagine. He should look about him, on the rare occasions when cars and lorries allow him to take a look. The only cheerful people I notice are all in highly-coloured advertisements, persuading us to buy something we don't really want.

I grumble if I don't get letters; I grumble if I do. If I am asked how I am, these days, I reply at once, 'Old, fat and gloomy'. I am the worst present-receiver in the County of

Warwickshire, for I can hardly manage a smile or a few pleasant words of thanks, and am obviously going to point out what is wrong with the present as soon as the giver is out of the room. In the unlikely event of receiving a gift horse, I would be spending hours examining its mouth, even if I didn't know what to look for. On all happy occasions—weddings, birthdays and the like— I am the shadow over the scene, probably muttering curses on the caterers. Few men have ever done more grumbling than I have. For writing I have a certain talent, but for grumbling I have indefatigable genius. True, I expect the worst, but when it is worse still, as it nearly always is, I am the loudest complainer. Go on a holiday with me—and you are doomed. My unconscious is busy attracting disappointment and disaster. At the bitter end, I am there to say, 'I told you so'.

Now then, how can any man, after offering such a dismal picture of himself, have the impudence to announce that he is also 'life-enhancing'? Well, to begin with, I think that impudence comes into it. A man can't be impudent and at the same time dreary and life-defeating, as far too many people are. He must have something that buoys him up, however pessimistic he may be. There must be a certain gusto somewhere. There must be energy to fuel all that loud complaining and grumbling, and people may find themselves responding to that energy. Again, deep in the pessimist's scene, lurking somewhere, must be some vision of what could be so much better if things were not so bad. It might be said that the optimist has this vision, right in the front of his mind. But that is not where it should be: it is liable to replace reality. And there is nothing life-enhancing about being unreal.

It is the pessimist, with his mocking smile, and not the optimist, with his insufferable cheery laugh, who really enjoys a sense of humour. He can laugh at himself—the supreme test, in my view —if only because he has a sense of proportion and understands the difference between what we want and what we get. He appreciates irony, both in his immediate circle and in the long tragic-farce of history. He doesn't wear his heart on his sleeve, like so many cheery loud laughers, but keeps it steadily pumping

[70]

away, deep in his breast, and is at once mocking yet compassionate, like another Cervantes. He may of course turn sour, as so many humorists have done in our age, often out of a wounded soft and enlarged ego; but if so, he will not have been from the beginning a pessimist, just a disappointed optimist.

I am trying to prove that there can be such a person—and call him a contradictory character, if you like—as a life-enhancing pessimist. I dare not go much further. It is for other people—who may or may not have plenty of evidence—to decide if I am life-enhancing. But I will add this. There may have been too much fault-finding, rumbling grumbling, loud denouncing of this, that and the other; but at least I have never been one of the huge, dim, conformist or apathetic multitude, advertisers' fodder, politicians' gulls, media mugs, all of them life-defeating, more than half-entangled in the death-wish. But then if I didn't think we now have too many of these types, I might not be a pessimist. And I am—and I enjoy it. So—quite possibly—life-enhancing.

XII

I have been thinking about my mid-teens, going back to 1910 and 1911. I was about to declare that there seemed to me no reason for doing this, but further reflection gave me one. At my age now everything is closing in; little that is new can be attempted; the shining lands of opportunity and golden promise have vanished; your friends are leaving you for the grave; you are living, not without bewilderment, in a repetitious Farewell. In the sharpest possible contrast to this is yourself in your middle teens, when you are out of childhood and seem to face the adult world, though as yet you don't really understand it, still keeping in mind certain magical elements really left over from childhood. You might be said to be staring at goldfields that are all mirages. You feel you have the possibilities of a giant when you are still only a dreaming dwarf. And if you have plenty of imagination, as I had, then it is all the more likely that you are ready to make an ass of yourself.

It was in those days, I well remember, that I was trying to decide between a glorious future as a writer (which excited me least), a musician or an actor. The musical choice was the most idiotic. I always saw myself conducting a symphony orchestra. (My delight in orchestras, even comparatively small theatre orchestras, was genuine, and lingers to this day.) I had no notion how I was to arrive with a baton in front of the Hallé (the one I knew best then) or the London Symphony: sorcery would have to be involved. I remember I did plod through two works on Harmony and Counterpoint without a glimmer of enthusiasm. (Naturally I was intellectually indolent then, and, to tell the truth, have been indolent ever since.) I played the piano a lot, but very badly, very badly indeed, being poorly taught and too lazy to practice. I had a fairly dashing right hand, but not intended for any careful listener, whereas my left hand never really co-operated and was very sketchy always. There were innumerable boys of ten who were better musicians than I was; I could no more read a full score than I could read Arabic; and yet I was daft enough to imagine that somehow or other, if I chose music, that baton would fall into my hand, and ninety men, all superb instrumentalists, would stare at me expectantly. I cannot imagine now why I should have thought for a moment that a musical career was open to me. Even at that age, it was daft. Not that some lads might not have achieved it, with sheer determination, iron application, a natural talent for the art. But certainly not young Jack Priestley.

(There is a certain amount of irony here. As I have explained elsewhere, so far as writing was concerned, I had no large vague daydreams at all, yet it was precisely as a writer, once I had made a beginning, that I showed sheer determination, and then and ever since I have genuinely been strong-willed.)

As for my possible choice of becoming an actor, it must be understood at once I hadn't *Hamlet* or *King Lear* in mind. I merely thought about going on the stage. (When at parties I amused girls my age, they were always saying, 'You ought to be on the stage.') I saw myself as some sort of comedian, perhaps for the next few years a 'light comedian', the type that sang chorus songs about the seaside. And indeed I actually bashed out a song about the seaside one Saturday night in the Bradford Mechanics' Institute. The impresario, if he deserves such a title, must have advertised for local artistes; and I can just remember being interviewed by a fruity old character, who, after solemnly feeling my bumps, like a phrenologist, engaged me for one performance and offered me a guinea—not a bad fee in those days for a teenager. Two of my maiden aunts were there that night, but not to see me, for I had been billed as *Jack Croly—from the Leading London and Provincial Halls*; and in fact they didn't recognize me behind the make-up. I remember I had another engagement, this time in broad daylight at a garden party, where I fascinated a girl called Ethel who had a saucy pout, dark eyes and curls, which I saw fairly often during the following months. All this was happening in 1910 or 1911, and as I recall it now I feel it might belong to some Victorian Dickensian world, not to the one that was shortly to disappear in the Great War. But I didn't persevere in my attempt to reach the stage, for it wasn't long before I switched to my writing self and landed a regular column in a local weekly as well as writing bad pseudo-mystical verse. However, after a solemn start on paper and in print, with the comedian in me temporarily submerged, that self came into his own at last—or so I prefer to believe—once I had established myself as a writer.

All this time, still in my mid-teens, I was playing soccer every Saturday, no longer for my school, which I had left, but for a side in a local league. In spite of being the youngest player in the side, I kept to my familiar position as full back, being pretty strong and heavy for my age. It could be rough going, though in those days we full backs didn't run about as much as they are expected to do now, generally keeping to our own half and being self-indulgent in the matter of vast spectacular clearance kicks, never really as useful as moving forward and directing sensible passes. On the other hand, we almost always avoided, by sharp twists, what I now find so maddening in the game, to wit, the endless passing back to the goalkeeper. (Soccer managers, please note.) But what made our league particularly rough was that it included several small mining towns or villages, where any gentlemanly nonsense about 'the best team winning' was completely ignored, so that often if we did win we had to run like hell for the pub we had used as a dressing-room. (Pubs were open all day then.) As there were no hot baths waiting for us in those pubs, we had to manage as best we could, with beer as an ally. Then, already feeling stiff, we might have a couple of long tramrides before we were near home. Yorkshire and Lancashire were famous in those days for long tramrides; and it was said that except for two or three blank miles you could go from Bradford to Blackpool by tram.

I loved this game of soccer and played it off and on until nearly the end of the First War, when I was no longer feeling fit to play. Nowadays, among the professionals, there are probably far more skills and a higher degree of fitness than there used to be; but even so, I feel that big money and publicity have brought tension into the game and a certain smooth ease has gone. Never visiting grounds any longer but occasionally watching a match on TV, I get the impression that the crowds of young fans are so busy drearily chanting or scuffling that they have no eye for the finer points of the game, especially for those long accurate passes that neatly split the opposite defence. I enjoyed playing but was entirely without ambition. Later, my attention was all on writing, and earlier, as I have said, I was divided between vague careers in music or acting. Through all these years leading up to the First War I had a good rich life that never cost me more than a few shillings. I have been described in a print as 'a Renaissance Man'. This is altogether too flattering. But I might claim to have been a Renaissance teenager, serving not a bad apprenticeship to a career in fiction and drama.

XIII

As a highly professional dramatist, with plays going all over the world, I have had a curious relationship with the Theatre. It might be said that I have seen both more of it and less of it than most professional dramatists. More of it because when actually working in the Theatre I have not been confined to the role of author but have played several other roles, as a director of two producing companies. I have seen less of it because, unlike many of my colleagues, when not actually working in the Theatre I keep away from it, being busy with other things. In other words, I have never led the life of a man of the Theatre, attending all important first nights or (in America) 'openings', entertaining at lunch or supper important actors or actresses, reading or listening to all the Theatre news and gossip. I can think of some people I have known who never seemed to get away from the Theatre, who ate it, drank it, breathed it, almost as if they never saw daylight. This has some professional advantages, bringing with it an expertise and a sense of theatrical fashion, but it lacks the nourishment to be had in the world outside the Theatre. If my plays have travelled far—as indeed they have—it may be that the best of them have gained from this nourishment, have brought something of the world outside on to the stage, have not been too theatrically theatrical.

However, I realize that, while reasonably helpful and considerate, I have never been a satisfactory person to work with in the Theatre. I can't come up with sufficient excitement. I am never bursting with enthusiasm. Something of that world outside remains with me. I look at critics' notices in terms of the box office—and that is all: the real Day of Judgment is still far away. But I am not proud of this detachment; I think it is wrong, rather lacking in empathy and imagination. For actors and

[76]

actresses are out there every night, displaying themselves, offering audiences their bodies, minds, personalities, and so they need, like so much oxygen, excitement and enthusiasm. They are quite right to demand something closer and warmer, backstage, than a cool appraisal. They are, so to speak, night after night half-naked in the market place. This is even more important to actors than it is to actresses, if only because they feel less security in their profession. I keep notes on all manner of subjects, and I find I have one on this subject that is worth quoting. Here it is.

Before I worked in the Theatre, which I did on and off for forty-five years, I thought that actresses would be far more troublesome and demanding than actors. This came to me from novels and press gossip, and experience soon told me it was completely wrong. Actresses were less troublesome and demanding, and far more loyal to the plays and productions. (But I don't mean to suggest that I have had a lot of trouble with actors.) The point is that actresses are much closer to ordinary natural women than actors are to the general run of men, from whom they can't help feeling they have separated themselves, so tend to feel uneasy and self-conscious. There are some professional men, notably lawyers and doctors, who have to do some acting as part of their day's work; but probably ninety-nine men out of every hundred never see themselves as potential actors. But most women are actresses of a sort, and quite a large number hug the belief they might have succeeded on the stage. The result is they feel far more at home in the Theatre than the men do, and consequently tend to behave better.

If I feel rather cool and detached about the Theatre we have now, this is not chiefly because I dislike the conditions in which it has to work, though I can't pretend to like them, but because I was spoilt by what happened in the 1930s, when my plays were first appearing. I had my own production company then, and was both the author and the boss man. I could finish a play, let us say, in June, and by August we would be rehearsing it, ready for the autumn season. (We were careful and rather artful about our costs of production too. For example, we would buy inexpensive secondhand furniture, when the set demanded it, instead of hiring what we wanted, as most producers did, and thereby paying for it ten times over.) Again, casting was so easy then compared with what happens now. If we wanted Jean Forbes-Robertson for *Time and the Conways* in London, then Jessica Tandy for New York, wonderful Jean and clever, attractive Jessica were what we got. But now what happens? This one is tied up with a TV series. That one has gone to the Royal Shakespeare Company, and the other one to the National; and as a taxpayer, supporting these companies, you are defeating yourself as a producer.

There must now be a very large number indeed of persons who belong officially to the Stage, some safely under contract, others living on bit parts or social security. But exceptional talent doesn't multiply as these numbers do, though I must add that the average level on TV, which is what I chiefly see these days, always seem to me fairly high, especially in small parts. (Nearly always I feel I am really looking at and listening to policemen, harassed housewives, waiters and barmen, cheeky shopgirls.) There are far more intelligent young men on the stage now than when I first started working in the Theatre. On the other hand, I seem to notice a shortage of quite remarkable girls, on their way to becoming leading ladies. But I could be going wrong here, if only because I go so rarely to the Theatre. This is partly due to the fact that nowadays I spend so few free evenings in London, and when I do have the time I find it more convenient, usually before dinner, to go to a cinema. If a film is disappointing, I just smoke and think about something else, whereas a play badly produced or poor in itself is sheer misery, so much discomfort and the waste of good money and an evening. And here I would add that the little art of sound construction—even in TV documentaries as well as in plays—is leaving us. Incidentally, the sneers at the 'well-made play' referred to its usual paltry content and not to its construction. (Nobody sneers at a well-made table.) And if there are too many loose messy new plays around, it is chiefly because they have been accepted too quickly and easily. Too few writers have been sent home to take another look at their third acts.

I suggest my *An Inspector Calls* is a well-made play. Just when you feel you have had enough of the Inspector's revelations, the surprises begin. That is why it has been performed all over the world. The Mermaid Theatre staged a very successful revival of it, with an excellent cast headed by Philip Stone as the Inspector. This revival had a far more enthusiastic reception, both by the press and the public, than the original star-studded production at the Old Vic in 1946. This was because the play had become more topical in feeling than it had been at the end of the war, when selfishness and callousness had been less evident. This is an interesting example of the way in which the fortunes of a play can be affected by a change in the public mood. The Mermaid was committed to its annual Christmas piece; otherwise the Inspector might have gone on playing to crowded houses for several more months.

In Manchester *Theatre 69* revived *Time and the Conways* in 1973–4, well directed but faulty in its casting. This was the only time, to my knowledge, that a play of mine was offered to large audiences all wrapped in blankets. It was during that grim period when theatres couldn't be properly heated, and this odd playhouse, put together within the enormous Cotton Exchange, was very cold indeed. So the management hired or bought hundreds of blankets and lent one to each member of the audience on arrival. I take it as a rare compliment to the play that there was nothing half-hearted and dismal about these blanketed audiences. Again, I couldn't help feeling that this piece about the ravages of passing time was more topical, closer to the public mood, than when it had been written in 1937. Further revivals, of varying quality, seem to me to have confirmed this.

I was not concerned directly with *The Good Companions* as a musical—the 'book' of which had been skilfully contrived by my friend Ronald Harwood—but of course I took a semi-paternal interest in it. The music and lyrics by André Previn and Johnny Mercer seemed to me—I came to know them well—very good indeed, quite exceptional; and if they were coolly received by some sections of the Press, I think it was because it was thought that two Americans shouldn't be involved in our very English *Good Companions.* In spite of one mistake in casting, with some charm missing, I enjoyed the show—and can still enjoy it on its excellent record—and the various audiences I saw it with seemed to love it. But it was not sensibly handled. After playing to enormous money at Her Majesty's for some months, it began to slip during the lean weeks after Christmas and was then whipped off to make room for another musical that proved to be a disaster. Had it been nursed for a few more weeks—as many a long-running musical has been—it would not only have run on and on but would also have been presented overseas. It remains in my mind as an ambitious and lovable musical that deserved more loyalty from its management.

Wondering what was happening abroad, I have just gone through my play agent's financial statements for the last few months. The result surprised me. Money has come in from Australia, Belgium, Czechoslovakia, France, Germany, Holland, Italy, Japan, New Zealand, Scandinavia, Spain and the U.S.A. Now there is no new dramatic material here. It is entirely a question of theatrical or TV performances of plays written 30 to 40 years ago. And what conclusion can I come to here? That I am already a classic? Perhaps not; but surely that I am at least halfway there, though I doubt if there are many people here in England who would put forward even that claim for me. This is the trouble about not being an out-and-out thorough-going Theatre man, just popping into it to do some work and then popping out again to take a look at the world. I am paying for some dubiety and detachment. But a freedom from fuss and silliness is well worth the price demanded. Or isn't it, remembering that my old love for the Theatre, an essential part of my youth, hasn't entirely vanished yet?

XIV

A friendly reviewer in *The Times* ends his notice by saying that my 'love of England and the English shines through the crusty prose and the crotchets.' Well, we shall now have some more crusty prose and crotchets. He is quite right of course: I love England and the English. I love England because for more than eighty years it has been my home; and I happen to believe in homes. No decent man would leave home because it might not cost so much living down the road. I may happen to think—as indeed I do—that taxation in England is far too high and is essentially foolish; but if I fled the country, to live in some alien place, I would feel I was damaging myself deep inside. I would be running away from love, inviting spiritual disaster. So many deep roots would be cut, I would feel ill-nourished and more than half-lost. England is my country, where I belong. Much of this is of course instinctive, hardly rational at all. I can love England and the English without particularly admiring them. I can even dislike a great deal that is typical of them. Many a man, with a mind of his own, stays at home, pays his whack, refuses to consider living anywhere else, but doesn't hesitate to grouse and grumble half the time. And that is this old crusty-prose-and-crotchet fellow: *Yours indignantly.*

To begin with, while England has produced its share—perhaps more than its share—of very clever men and women, its general level is chiefly marked by stupidity. I may be prejudiced here, but it does seem to me that there are more stupid people here, some of them in high places, than there are in most West European countries. I never visit these without feeling that there are more intelligent people around, fewer wooden-headed chumps. If we are half-ruined now, as we appear to be, I feel it is entirely our own fault. We have done it ourselves, without any sinister plotting abroad. If I had behaved as the nation has done, I would have gone bankrupt some years ago and would have had some very sharp things said to me, all about spending more than I earned. And no blame attached either to the Tory Party or the Labour Party would have been allowed, the frequent excuse of our politicians, busy passing the buck. Private stupidity is cemented into public stupidity, stiffened by the appointment of whole armies of bureaucrats, civil servants, advisers, all at vast expense. This calls for murderous taxation, now perhaps the highest in the world. Not being sentimental old codgers like me, a lot of bright chaps escape this taxation by leaving the country, so that intelligence is lost and stupidity gains another victory.

It is in England where heads of nationalized industries, faced with rising costs, don't behave like sensible business men and try to find more customers, to earn more, but raise their charges and cut their services. This brings them in even less, and of course hurts the public. At the same time we have professional politicians, supposed to be in their right minds, who tell us we should not have less of this but more and more of it, handing over banks and insurance companies to the same elaborate mismanagement. Our forefathers, if they had heard such advice, so many short cuts to chaos, would have stoned these fellows in the streets; but we are made of dimmer softer stuff.

It is in England where the lowest standards of public food and service are tolerated, as they would never be in any other country in Western Europe. The same people who are lazy at work are also lazy-minded, ready to accept anything without any protest when they are trying to enjoy themselves. So mess, squalor and muck can be found everywhere, often making fat profits. There was a time—and I remember it—when local standards of living had to be lowered when going abroad, the poor foreigners not being up to them; but now the English fly abroad to look at some fresh paint, bright-faced service, and something fit to eat. All this has happened since the Second War, to which the English gave all they had, only to slip and slide afterwards, whether as shop stewards bent on over-manning and restrictive practices or as housewives living out of tins. Meanwhile, governments behave

[82]

like irritable and bossy nannies, demanding more and more power to make people good and safe, and quietly moving towards a totalitarian state, leaving the citizenry less and less room to make its own choices. And people who are treated like so many babies will soon become as irresponsible and messy as babies. Hence the lowered standards.

It is in England where if sex is mentioned in connection with any public figure, the country promptly goes out of its mind. The media cannot contain themselves. The topic is flogged to death. Molehills are transformed into mountains of cant and humbug. A foreigner would imagine that sex, in its least attractive aspects, had just been discovered. It is on these occasions, not at all rare, that I feel ashamed of my fellow countrymen and wish they would either grow up or shut up. Moreover—all this at a time when probably about a fifth of the nation are so steeped in sex they might be living in a squalid Venusberg. Here is a country where a lot of working men, leaving their wives to cook the Sunday dinner, go to the nearest club to watch strip-tease; and where the newspapers with the largest circulations discover and reveal female anatomy almost every morning. So why all these shocking revelations? Are public men supposed to be eunuchs or hermaphrodites? Or is *envy* at work, as it has been behind some political decisions?

Again, there is now too much ideology gnawing away at what used to be the basic English character. We were famous once for our political pragmatism, our realistic outlook, our broad toleration of opposing views. No doubt the common run of the English people are not so very different. But it is not they who make the most noise nowadays. The ideologists, knowing their own rules and quite blind to what other people are really like, now pop up all over the place. Once we kept clear of Marxism, leaving it to foreigners who knew no better, but now the Marxists find their way into innumerable executive councils and committees, gaining power by their unmatched ability to bore the hell out of fellow members, who depart, yawning, leaving the hard core to pass its Marxist resolutions. Some of these castiron ideologists ought to be compelled to spend at least six months in countries where Marx and Lenin are the only patron saints and stifling boredom is a national product.

Finally, the people who are out of luck in modern England are authors. Victorian England liked its authors, bought their books, applauded every appearance they made. But those days have gone. Bookshops and bookbuyers are harder to find now in England than in most West European countries. The official English either despise or detest authors and do as little as possible to promote their welfare. The very men who will make pompous after-dinner speeches, praising 'Our Literary Heritage', will rush to pass measures screwing the last penny out of authors and have delayed the Public Lending Right year after year. There are countries in which the public atmosphere is favourable to authorship. Now I have been a professional writer for over half a century, and always I have envied my foreign colleagues. Compared with us, they were nourished and cherished. Consider this. When the Public Lending Right was first mooted, out came the librarians—really to announce that they hated us authors. If we were dissatisfied with the rewards of our profession, some librarians suggested, we had better try to earn our living some other way, possibly with a steady job at the gasworks. I don't think that in fifty years I have ever had a letter of thanks and appreciation from a librarian. They were waiting to let fly at us as soon as a Public Lending Right was suggested. It is only dead authors who attract any kind words in England.

So there you have it. Some crusty prose and crotchets about England and the English. Yet it is still quite true that I love England and the English. What would not be true is that I am *in love* with them, seeing them shining in a misty radiance, like the girls—in my case—of long ago. There is no infatuation here. I stand by England because it is my home. I have an abiding affection for the English because in a sense they are all my brothers and sisters and cousins and aunts and uncles. But then what do we think, in an hour of candour, about the homes we have had and the relatives that have gone along with them? Something surely that calls for some crusty prose and a few crotchets. So for these, I make no apology.

XV

I have been groping in my memory towards my earliest child-hood. It has taken me back into the nineteenth century, nearer in time to *David Copperfield* than it is to myself here, remembering and writing. I am being held up among a mysterious company of large adults in Blackpool, though how I realized, at such an age, we were in Blackpool, I can't imagine. I am sitting on my grandfather's knee in a horse-bus and I am fascinated by the thick straw on the floor, it being winter. I am being scolded by an elderly housekeeper because I have been naughty, kicking over a can of paint. The housekeeper is there because I have no mother. (Later, I acquired, against all tradition, a stepmother who was kind and gentle and mothered me as best as she could.) I never set eyes on my mother, who must have died just after I was born. Nobody ever spoke to me about her: there was—as there often is in such situations—a strict conspiracy of silence. It is a fact that I know only two things about her, namely, that she was witty and that she was once turned out of a theatre because she laughed out loud at the wrong moment. Her photograph survives and I am far more like her than I am like my father. He was a fair to gingerish, blue-eyed, round-headed type, very much a decent public-spirited citizen but apt to be hot-tempered and rather violent in his domestic life; whereas I have a longer head and face, am darker and have grey-blue eyes, and have never kept a loose trigger on my temper.

The loss of a mother meant that it was impossible that I should have a happy earliest childhood. There were areas of dark bewilderment. Something was missing that should have been there. I was out of luck too at my infant school. The woman I remember there obviously disliked me, possibly, I fancy now, because she disliked my father, who had taught once, on the junior level, at that same school. I can just recall that stupid woman's face, square and for ever frowning in my direction, as I remember my own terror and despair, at an age when you don't realize that time may soon change everything, when you feel small, helpless and apparently doomed, arriving day after day with fear curdling your inside. I call that woman stupid because she can't have had any imagination at all and was really unfitted to be in charge of young children. A mother, I feel, realizing soon what was happening to me, would have marched straight up to that woman and told her what she was doing to me. But there was no mother. By the time I had my kind and gentle stepmother, I was out of that infant class and was turning into a boy, out of those dark areas into some sunlight, beginning to enjoy my passion for books and games, doing well at school in all things, actually winning medals for sport—medals, like those belonging to the First War, that have all mysteriously vanished.

One little incident, not without a touch of symbolism, has stayed in my memory, though I think I must have been about five at the time. In warm sunshine I was sitting or lying on a small grassy mound. Not idly dreaming at all, fully awake, I felt very strongly that somewhere underneath me, hidden in that mound, was a great and marvellous treasure. I hadn't the least desire to dig it up. All that mattered was that it was there and that I knew it was there. I realized with sudden joy that I shared a secret with the earth below. I never told anybody. And now, at least seventy-five years later, I am enjoying those moments again. Perhaps it is no coincidence that among my favourite words in my work—and almost all writers have their favourites—are *magic* and *magical*. I am, you might say, still perched on that mound.

Even in my eighties, they are with me yet, those influences of early childhood. Over and over again, I realize now, I have written as if something terribly important could be missing from the life I have been describing, something lost that ought to be there, a loss that could only be made good by magic. I have been praised for commonsense, when in fact I have very little. My adult *persona* has always been misleading. Inside I am somebody quite different, never really feeling secure with myself. (If I have worked so hard, it has not been for fame or money but *to justify my dubious existence.*) Though not exactly a coward—and indeed, surgeons and dentists, who ought to know, have said I am a brave man—I am to this day constantly and sharply apprehensive, a small child in yet another dark area: the worst, I feel, can easily happen. Though hardly modest in many respects, nevertheless I am always surprised when I am told that somebody likes me.

I welcome all mysteries and marvels; I am at heart a persistent crackpot. So I detest all those complete systems that explain everything away, leaving us with a lot of machinery and grey dust. Joy comes flooding in when it looks as if two and two might make five. Instead of classics, which might have educated me, I was taught science at school, and have forgotten it all, though probably it was wrong anyhow. But though always hoping for the miraculous, there lingers in me a certain scepticism, probably because I was brought up in the West Riding, one of the citadels of the tough-minded. So I tend to cancel out, neither believing nor entirely disbelieving; but this leaves me at home with literature, in which types like me are common enough. (Number One is Shakespeare.) Incidentally, my politics are based almost entirely on compassion. When the working classes faced long hours and low wages, I was always on their side, even if some of their employers refused to buy my books or theatre seats. Now that the middle classes risk extermination, I am one of their loyal supporters. At the core of my political belief is the feeling that if we lose a reasonable liberty, we are lost indeed, turning into so many robots.

I have declared more than once that I have turned from one literary form to another just because I have had so many different ideas begging to be used. This is not altogether a thumping lie: some truth remains. But it is also true that the influences of my childhood have been at work here too. Secretly I have been unsure of myself, not risking to stand or fall by any one form of writing, shifting my ground rather than defending it with all the force I possessed. And it seems to me that in this matter I have had better luck than I deserved to have, far better than many more courageous and determined writers have had, their work not having gone so far round the world as some of mine has. And indeed I would say that I have been more fortunate in my life than I might have expected from such a childhood and its legacy of apprehension. But what—I ask myself now—was that great and marvellous treasure that was lying beneath me when I was on that mound, at the end of the last century. Did I win it or lose it? I don't know. Just as there was so much in my earliest childhood that I didn't understand, so too, all along the way, there has been a great deal that has been beyond my comprehension.

XVI

The *Book of Quotations* I have just been consulting carries eighty-eight closely-printed columns on Death in all its aspects. There is a lot of showing-off and striking attitudes here. The Old Testament offers the best value: for example, *He shall return no more to his house, neither shall his place know him any more.* That has the right heart-shaking ring, reminding me that all the men who were old friends are dead and gone: not one is left to share some late-night talk and drink. And all we know for certain is this sense of loss. One man can tell us all about the later Roman Empire, but he doesn't know what we want him to know. Another man has discovered in far space a *black hole* that might swallow a thousand suns, but it is useless to ask him what is to happen to Aunt Mary now in intensive care. Yet another man juggles with unimaginable particles but stares as blankly at death as the cowman at the nearest farm. We are compelled to perform, without any re-hearsal, in a huge tragic farce.

But would it be any better if we knew everything, with little illustrated booklets and special TV documentaries (*Death and Afterwards*) for children? No, it would be even worse. The final dignity would be removed from us. We would be knowing and vulgar, or just bored, at our deathbeds and over our coffins. A great mystery, perhaps the last, would be gone for ever. We would have to face more and more yawning routine. There would never be another surprise. Apathy, bad enough now among large sections of our people, would be vastly increased and deepened. Not always as considerate as He promised to be, God has done us a kindness here, by keeping something hidden, preserving a mystery.

Nevertheless, having said this, I still feel we are entitled, in our common human weakness, to try occasionally to twitch aside the veil, to indulge in what must obviously be guesswork. Is death the end? Can there be an After-life? And if there can, what would it be like? Of course it may be better not to ask such questions, as most people probably refuse to do. But if we ask them and yet shrink from sending at least a few guesses in their direction, we are spiritless creatures. So there will be some guesses from me, not necessarily wild and an insult to the intelligence, but possibly, it seems to me, quite reasonable. But let us see.

First, I can't pretend to cope with those earnest and sturdy believers, who are sure that after some period of complete rest the Last Trump, or some other alarm device, will bring them out of their graves, with newly resurrected bodies, to await final judgement, taking them to bliss, torment, or that Limbo which is about what most of us deserve. I don't know what will happen but I can't accept this particular scenario. However, I fancy that such believers are in a minority in Western Europe or America. My guess is that now most people think that death brings complete extinction. Perhaps about half of them welcome this thought. They have had enough of life, with all its aches and pains, worry and fuss, strain and stress, and will be glad when it is all blotted out, once and for all. The other half are secretly terrified, and so banish all talk of death and dying, unlike the more robust Victorians, who had far less progress at work on them. Guessing again, I would say that this division—with extinction accepted on both sides—takes care of nineteen out of every twenty of our neighbours.

Some beliefs in an After-life are so silly that I propose to ignore them. But that doesn't mean I accept the familiar case for extinction. It is all too easy to be bullied and bounced into that. Along comes Dr Knowall and defies you to prove that life survives death. But this is the wrong way round. It is up to him to prove that it doesn't. It is he who has made the dramatic and extraordinary statement, that life is anything but continuous, that total breaks with it are common events, that a weak heart or a faulty kidney can be totally destructive of mind and personality. It is not Dr Knowall who is being reasonable, nor is it you, if you object to him, who are being a weak dreamer. Are you as a person simply an effect of your body, like a certain way of walking? Do we say I *am* a body or I *have* a body? Even beautiful women, intensely aware of their alluring bodies, still say they *have* a body. Sooner or later we might meet one who tells us she had a nice dead body. And if this seems too steep, let us remember all those well-authenticated out-of-the-body experiences that have been carefully described scores of times. Nor should we forget the suggestion, not without some degree of proof, that there exists in us *a second system*, close to the old idea of the etheric body, that might well survive death.

However, the opponents of survival—we might call them the *extinctionists*—have their own strong case. If mind and personality survive, where is our evidence? Yes, indeed, the spiritualists claim to have established regular communication with some happy land beyond the grave; but most of us find this hard to accept. A long procession of noble and powerful minds, who would have been eager to explain what had happened to them, has wound its way into the darkness of death, and these great men have told us nothing. If communication with the living had been possible and desirable, these are the very men who would have made use of it. But not one reliable message has come from them. Either no communication is possible, or the light of wonderful minds, a Plato or an Aristotle, a Shakespeare or a Bacon, was snuffed out as if they had been so many guttering candles. On this ground, the victory of death cannot be challenged. When our time runs out, we are extinguished for ever. Our fate then is worse than that of the most cruelly hunted animal. We have to live as best we can with the thought—unless of course we accept the idea of a loving God who will take care of our immortal souls —that sooner or later, with all our aspirations shattered, with every dream gone, we are to be blotted out, only continuing to exist, at best, in a few fading memories. We behave badly all too often in this life, but as we move through it under a sentence of death, it is surprising we are not much worse and do assemble a little decency.

I was asked in a TV interview if I were afraid of death. I said I wasn't but was afraid of doctors. I meant by that of course that I dreaded being kept alive with all dignity lost, a semi-conscious vegetable. I can't find in myself any deep-seated fear of extinction—even though I have just been rather eloquent on the subject—or of whatever kind of existence survival might bring me. My argument for survival seems to me intellectual and not emotional. Perhaps I ought to add here that in psychic affairs I am the opposite of a sensitive, I am *a thick*. I can never remember having the feeling that anybody who had died was still very close to me, or that any communication from beyond the grave was reaching me. But even so, I have always had some strange and memorable dreams, and one of them deserves to be described in this place.

Edward D. was a close friend right from our Cambridge years. He died—and not an easy death—three or four years ago. Not very long afterwards he appeared in one of my unusually vivid and memorable dreams. I was in a fairly large room and a number of people entered. I didn't recognize any of them; they were just dream supernumeraries. But then my dear friend Edward came in. Clearly he was shy, hesitant, not sure of a welcome; not behaving at all as he would have done in life. I crossed to him at once, put a hand on his shoulder—and even after waking I could still feel the rough tweed of his coat—and told him warmly how glad I was to see him. That was the end of the dream, though it had taken more time than my description suggests, his entrance and hesitation being almost in slow motion, with no attempt on his part to catch my eye, as if he felt he had no right to join this company.

Here I must confess I am not prepared to interpret this dream. If it were anybody else's I would probably have a shot at it. I have noticed this with the symbolism in my own creative work. My attention has usually to be called to it by a sensitive friend, almost always feminine, who having discovered the symbols would make some attempt to interpret them, so far as that is possible. But the dream does seem to suggest a point made by Jung in his chapter *On Life After Death*. This is that if such life exists, it is not, as many people appear to imagine, *superior* in any way to our ordinary life before our death, the survivors not being in any way wiser and stronger than we are but in fact—if any fact can be involved here—are more anxious to learn from us than to teach us anything. We might say that life before death is the *thing*, where much may be learnt or created, and that life after death is a mere quivering shadow of that thing. And after all, this is more or less how many ancient peoples, notably some of the Greeks, concluded it must be.

Having argued in favour of survival, I feel I can't escape making a guess or two at what life after death might be like. (It would not go on for ever: nothing does, I feel.) There would, I fancy, be no marked change in the mind and personality that had survived, both of them shaped and coloured before death. Using a far less substantial body fashioned out of our *second system*, our old etheric friend, this other life, possibly four-dimensional, would seem to us now like a dream life. Here I am not suggesting any glow of happiness, desires miraculously satisfied, but simply the scope and texture of the experience. It might be thin and shadowy compared with our life before death, where we really create the selves that have survived the grave. Possibly a large part of this new life might be a repetition of what had happened before. (I have always had a rather grim fancy—and even based a TV play on it—that suicides, desperate to escape for ever, find themselves repeating their hours of despair and the fatal decision to take their own lives.) But would we encounter beyond the grave the people we have loved? Possibly we might if they decided, so to speak, to dream the same dream. Again, there is the possibility of recapturing former peak experiences, great moments in art as well as in love. We may enter another dimension of time in which all events continue to exist. Even so, I must return to my point that what is all-important is how we live here and now, what we make while we are still able to be makers (a happy home will do), before we squeeze through the narrow door of death into the land of dreams and shadows.

But, finally, do I know what I am talking about? Strictly speaking, the answer is No. What else could it be? All I can do is offer a few guesses. But let us not go, taking the sap and juice out of our lives, in fear of Death.

[93]

XVII

How do novelists create their characters? I know from experience
that readers often pose this question. And indeed many of them
are ready to answer it themselves. Their guesses tend to arrive at
extremes. The novelist, they fancy, either wildly invents everybody or copies directly from life. There are no fine shades in their
idea of character-creation. And this is quite wrong, as I propose
to show from what I can remember of my own work in fiction.
But there will be no systematic examination of that work. (I would
never have started writing this book if I had been asked to be
systematic anywhere in it.) As novels of mine and their characters
come to mind, I will report, as honestly as I can, on the creative
processes involved in them. People who don't know some of the
novels mentioned are entitled to skip. People who have never
read a single one of them might as well close this book now: they
have never been interested in me, and I am not interested in
them. Regular readers, loyal souls, are my audience here.

Let us begin with the famous, notorious, probably insufferable
Good Companions. Two of the three chief characters in this
picaresque tale, Inigo Jollifant and Miss Trant, are complete
inventions, though on quite different lines, Miss Trant being a
modest low-profile invention while Inigo is a cheeky loud one.
I have never met an Inigo Jollifant, and am not sorry. Jess Oak-
royd, however, is partly drawn from life, the artisan-father of a
schoolfriend of mine being the model. Though this man had none
of Jess's romantic *wanderlust* urges, they looked alike and often
talked in the same fashion. Among the characters in the concert
party and those encountered in its travels I imagine there were a
few partly based on types I had run across myself; but now I
have forgotten which they were.

Angel Pavement is a far more realistic novel, yet, surprisingly

nough, not one of its chief characters—Turgis, Smeeth, Golspie
nd his daughter, Miss Matfield—is even partly based on a live
model: they are all inventions. So are the Dersinghams, but then
hey are drawn from some large pool of comic-pathetic middle-
lass London types. However, Mr Golspie is something else, and
wes his vitality perhaps to a certain brutal streak in myself.
I remember meeting, out at lunch, Elizabeth (Countess Russell),
vho looked a pretty doll of a woman but had plenty of character
nd a sharp mind of her own, and she told me she *adored* Mr
Golspie, just the kind of man for her.) However, the chief charac-
er in *Angel Pavement* is really London itself.

Nobody has mentioned *Faraway* to me for a great many years,
nd it must be almost forgotten, though when it first appeared
I. G. Wells and Somerset Maugham went out of their way to
raise it. I didn't put much of myself or of anybody else into its
rincipal characters—William Dursley, the Commander, Mr
Lamsbottom—but then I don't—and didn't—see it as a novel of
haracter for it is much closer to a tale (symbolic, though) of
dventure and far travel. (It even took me to Tahiti.) I have never
pplied myself to it simply as a reader—as I have done with a
ew other novels—and so cannot remember what exactly hap-
ened to such characters as it has. I do recall that work on it
vas disturbed by various events in my private life, and this cannot
ave done it much good, no matter what Wells and Maugham
ound to praise in it. Now that I have reached an age when I can
muse myself by reading myself, I must try this longish and fairly
mbitious tale and discover how it reads after forty-five years.
Iowever, I am certain it will not seem a triumph of character-
reation.

Bright Day, which I have re-read, is a very different matter.
t has been generally considered to be my best novel, and it was
ncluded in the *Everyman Library* as a kind of modern classic, I
uppose. Its central figure and narrator, Gregory Dawson, had
vorked in a wool office in the West Riding before becoming a
rofessional writer, and as this is what I had done too it can
asily be assumed there is a considerable autobiographical element
ere. Well, there is—and there isn't. There is because the early

[95]

background is not unlike my own, and various figures that appear in it are more or less sketched from memory. And no doubt I put a little of myself into Gregory Dawson, but there is no attempt at a self-portrait. I never knew 'a magic family' like the Alingtons and they themselves together with everything that happened to them are all inventions. Again, Gregory's career as a writer involved as he was with films, is quite different from my own even though I have written occasional films. His various stages of disillusion are not borrowed from my own life. (The more or less 'happy ending' has been criticized as an artistic blemish, the narrative being forced out of its natural key and tone; and I accept this criticism.) What gives the novel such strength and depth as it has are the construction and the various convincing time-shifts. What I share with Gregory Dawson is a deep-seated nostalgia for that golden haze of youth before the First War, and against the loss of all that shining promise he cries out with my voice. So in this particular respect here is a leading character created out of myself.

Looking back, I realize now I should have delayed publication of *Festival at Farbridge*. I was in favour of a Festival of Britain not for political but for psychological reasons. After years of austerity, it was time we cheered ourselves up. But a large section of the Press disliked the Festival idea because they regarded it as an attempt by an unpopular Labour government to curry favour. And as my novel was enthusiastically pro-Festival it was very coolly received by the section of the Press. If I had delayed publication, so that this big crowded novel, very much in the comic tradition, escaped any political bias, it would have succeeded better then and would not, I suspect, have been rather under rated ever since. Re-reading it quite recently, I decided that it was longer than it need have been—I did go on and on a bit—but that much of its humour has outlasted mere topicality. Of its three chief characters, I would say that Laura is a fair sketch of a lively girl, Theodore is a stick, and Commodore Tribe, the genial charlatan, really works. So does the energetic and perspiring Captain Mobbs, a complete invention, not based on anybody. But in the crowded scene, though not lost in it, is the only

[96]

character I remember that I took directly from life, in every particular; and I know as a fact that the original never recognized himself.

Lost Empires is completely dominated by Richard Herncastle, the painter who tells this story of his youth on the Halls, and his Uncle Nick, the illusionist. Neither of these is a portrait of anybody. They are both invented characters but with touches of myself in them. On the other hand, some of the people they meet along the way are more or less sketch-portraits from memory. Perhaps I ought to add that this novel cuts much deeper into life than I realized when I was writing it, containing as it does a certain amount of symbolism first indicated to me, across the Atlantic, by our friend Evelyn Ames, herself a good writer. Any curious reader should consider the relation between young Herncastle, the honest aspiring artist, and the technically efficient Uncle Nick, the cynical illusionist; and then turn some attention on to the dwarfs in the narrative. However, I offer no prize for any symbolic interpretation.

Among my minor novels, I think my favourite is *Sir Michael and Sir George*, with their rival arts councils. (It is a favourite too with my wife, once a civil servant.) Sir George begins very much as a type but turns into a genuine character before we have done with him. His rival, Sir Michael, trapped in the end by the force of his imagination, was not modelled on anybody known to me, and has nothing of myself in him, though I would not say his cool philandering, before he falls in love, was entirely invented. There are, as far as I can recall, no portraits from life among their staffs. But the artful, if rather lovable, Tim Kemp does owe something, both in his appearance and style of talk, to a certain Tommy P. whom I used to meet, as a fellow-reviewer in a Fleet Street pub, back in the 1920s. However, I can't imagine Tommy plotting as cunningly as Tim Kemp does.

As I have said elsewhere, my first favourite among all my novels, long or short (it is the longest) is *The Image Men*. It would be easy for me to declare that its sharply contrasted two heroes— and to me they *are* heroes—are complete inventions; but it would be untrue. Possibly I regard them with such affection because I

[97]

put a lot of myself into them. To a limited degree there is an authoritative side to my character, and there is also—perhaps to a less degree, perhaps not—a persuasive and rather seductive side. So I took these two traits, enlarged and decorated them, and created the commanding Professor Saltana and the artful and pleasing Dr Tuby. And just as this is my favourite novel, so these two are my favourite characters. After 300,000 words I felt compelled to leave them—with a tremendous unabashed happy ending—and I did it with deep regret. With all their impudent adventures—among academics, media types, business men, senior politicians—I had given myself a well-earned holiday. I hope a host of readers have caught and enjoyed the spirit of it, though I shall be surprised if there are not more men than women among them, sustained satire being closer to masculine taste.

Even so, I take a pride in my two leading women—the sensible and ample Elfreda and the half-timid, half-cheeky, large-eyed Lois. I realize only too well that the women in my earlier novels were poor examples of character-creation, being either pretty images or mere comic sketches. In addition to Elfreda and Lois, the women in *The Image Men* are all far better, genuine characters. And the sex throughout seems to me about right. You know what's happening in the bedrooms without having to undress everybody. There is a proper distinction between serious relationships and rather casual impudent adventures. It is of course impossible to please everybody in this department, especially if you have an audience of different ages and styles of life, as I trust I still have. All you can do, it seems to me, is to please yourself first and then hope you have some luck.

Within the limits of a shortish comic novel, *Found, Lost, Found: or The English Way of Life*, I don't think I did too badly with its central character, Tom Dekker. He drinks too much gin, steadily without getting drunk, because he is bored, both inside and outside his Ministry. He is better than a type, possessing wit and humour, but undoubtedly the type exists, men whose chief enemy is not strain or stress but boredom. We may assume that his Kate, a firm character behind her belief, probably idiotic, that she can write plays, will put an end to most of this boredom.

[98]

She knows that Tom is much cleverer than she is but also realizes that she is the more stable character. I don't think I could have done much more with Kate but I could have run to greater length with Tom if I had not planned, in the first place, a cheeky short comic novel.

How are characters created? I have never discussed this with a fellow novelist; I can only answer for myself and then add a few guesses. Very superficial characters, probably quick sketches from life, can be dismissed: there is no mystery in their production. But substantial characters of some depth must involve the co-operation of the unconscious, and this at once brings in a magical element. These characters take possession of their writers, often behaving as they please, defying any plan or synopsis, revealing unsuspected traits as people so often do in real life. And indeed a complete consistency of behaviour suggests that no major character of memorable stature has been created. If the novelist himself has been surprised, then so much the better. The unconscious has been at work as it always has in dreams. Perhaps a major character might be compared to an enduring dream figure.

However, there is another way of looking at character-creation. Let us say I am brooding over a novel long before I have written a single word of it. I feel that my root idea demands a certain kind of character, who comes into my brooding. At first he is only a distant acquaintance. More brooding brings him nearer, and soon I seem to know a lot more about him: I see him, hear him, begin to understand him; he is now somebody I know very well indeed, almost a close friend, even though I may not particularly like him. At this point, as I have suggested earlier, I may even inject something of myself into him. With empathy now building up, I may now have here a character fit to play a major part in my novel.

Most male creative writers have a considerable feminine element in their psyche. This probably makes them just about as observant as the average woman is, even if they may appear to be dreamily detached or absent-minded in company. They are not there taking notes but they know, on most occasions, what is

[99]

going on. This may have been happening since childhood. (Dickens here is an excellent example.) Like a man for ever adding to his deposit account at the bank, the novelist will have salted away a great store of observant memories that may pass from consciousness into the enduring vaults of the unconscious, which will reveal its treasures when pressure is put upon it because the novelist is now at work. Then situations, scenes, and, above all, characters emerge and come to life. Apart from the actual choice of words, this can be at its best an effortless process. But before we envy the good novelist his luck, we must remember that for years and years, and on innumerable occasions, when most men may have been only half-attending to what has been said and done, he may have been fully alive, missing nothing. Life, like any normal woman, repays us generously if we offer it our close attention. And if, as writers, we want to create living characters, we must take care not to be only half-alive ourselves. While there must be no failure of imagination, there must also be no lack of energy, as all the masters have shown us.

THE HAPPY DREAM

An ESSAY

For Jacquetta

NOTE: This was published in the early Spring of 1976, as a limited signed edition, a very handsome little volume, by the excellent Whittington Press.

The text here is exactly the same. But I have added some Afterthoughts.

ONE

Consider the following. 'She lives in a dream world.' 'He was always a dreamer.' 'They were dreaming half their time.' It seems clear to me that the dreams here are not those that rise out of sleep and the night. They are daydreams, hazily put together by the ego in its idlest moments, all too often for self-glorification. The youth saves that haughty girl from fire or drowning. Years later he sees himself being sent for by the Chairman of the Board, to be congratulated and promoted. Then, a neglected elder, a message from Downing Street arrives at his fireside: he is to be honoured at last. This is daydreaming.

Now I have always had a wide and greedy appetite—but not for the lotus. For some reason I am not ready to provide, I have never been a daydreamer. On and off for sixty-five years I have tried to use my imagination, but always in a positive outgoing manner, never to saunter through or loll in sagas that glorified J.B.P. I can't attribute this to modesty, having always had a good opinion of myself; and indeed I suspect it is the daydreamer, busy with his foolish fantasies, awarding himself prizes conjured out of the air, who is the victim of too much modesty, of a poor opinion of himself outside his dream world. But I also think he suffers from a slackness and lethargy of the will, a reluctance to face the glare and din of the arena; incidentally, a weakness of which most females, trying to sort out the men they attract, are sharply aware. So many habitual daydreamers tend to drift into a realm of compliant but dim goddesses, a masturbatory world.

To move from daydreams to the true dreams that arise unbidden from sleep and the night is almost like a change of country. But of course our night dreams can vary enormously in character and quality. Here I quarrel with some of the sleep-researchers who have been hard at it these last few years. I do this when they announce that dreams are simply the brain's garbage disposal, a ragbag of unwanted odds and ends, a swilling out of the day's rubbish. People who believe this have lived so far in a much duller world than the one I know. Their nights have gone without illumination. Profound experiences have been denied them, which may explain why they have volunteered to sit up with sleep-research units.

While we may have thousands of rubbish dreams, forgotten as soon as we open our eyes, we may be allotted a share of memorable dreams, which we may be able to describe almost exactly, even after years. (Several pieces of mine are in fact descriptions of such dreams, with nothing added for dramatic or humorous effect.) These dreams, which may bring us anything from terror to a rich absurdity, seem to me to belong to a different order of dreaming. They do not come from the ragbag or rubbish disposal depart-ment, always offering us the instantly forgettable. They seem to me to be definite creations just as a produced play or a film is a definite creation. They include what is necessary and leave out what is unnecessary. If colour is important, then they are in colour; but if black-and-white will do, then they are content with that. They can keep us solitary or take us into crowds, according to the theme that is being developed. If it suits their purpose they can turn a person we know into several persons or, reversing the process, can cram two or three personalities into one dream character. And of course they have sufficient scenery at their disposal to bankrupt all the world's leading theatrical companies. The variety, the breadth and depth, the sheer speed of their creativity make anything we can do consciously look like tup-pence. The walls and floors dissolved by sleep reveal a world of marvels. Have we any freehold here or is it all on a temporary brief lease? What a cruel stroke to extinguish us before we can become more closely acquainted with this limitless creative abund-ance, when we have had only rare glimpses of its marvels! But to this I will return later, when the heart cries out at its exile from a happy dream.

Not every kind is represented in my dream repertory. For example, I have never had recurring dreams, which many people know only too well. I have not had any of them described in detail to me, but I cannot help suspecting there is something sinister about this repetition. What is going on in the dream factory down below? Is the recurrence a warning? Have we here something like repeated S.O.S. signals? Is the dreamer in danger? Or is he in need of night medicine that he must take in one dose after another until his psyche is feeling better? However, there is no point in my asking questions of this sort when I cannot supply any answers. I am glad to report that I have never had any recurring dreams; and I hope I do not start any now in my old age—*except for one*.

Another sort that is absent—at least within adult memory—is that old favourite of many night adventurers—the erotic dream. I have made love only in waking hours. No eager shapely girls come smiling out of the dark to reveal their charms, to open arms and legs. Is this because I am prudish, severely chaste? On the contrary. It is because I have been lusty and given to lechery and have never hidden my inclinations from my waking self. In other words, nothing has ever been suppressed in this department. Never a sexy inclination has been hurried out of consciousness. This does not mean that my waking life has been one long orgy—far from it—but at least it does mean that I have never been busy stoking the unconscious with a heated sexuality forbidden to consciousness. Therefore no wildly erotic dreams have come bursting out from below. I have come to terms with Eros while awake, so that, not neglected and furious, she has not had to burst into my dreams. (Don't write to me about that 'she' for Eros, because, defying the old mythology, I prefer to see Eros as essentially feminine, and indeed the heart and soul of the feminine principle.)

Looking back on my remembered dreams, I see they have had their special times, never arriving regularly. I recall very little from childhood. (Mine was not unhappy: I was out of literary fashion from the start.) There was something like a nightmare, when I was about ten, for a favourite uncle appeared in the doorway, very angry, glaring at me; and this turned out to be precognitive, because years later, when I was on leave during the First War, I suddenly caught sight of him, across the length of a bar, and there he was, very angry, glaring at me. (But here I must stop for I have described this dream elsewhere, as indeed I have described in one place or another most of the dreams I remember best.) However, just a word in passing about precognitive dreams, dealt with at length in my *Man and Time*. I cannot remember having had one since I wrote that book, though it is quite possible that I may have missed half-a-dozen. They can be tricky to spot if you are not in search of them, as Dunne himself pointed out nearly fifty years ago.

I can remember only one dream out of my four-and-a-half years in the army. Later, however, about the time I was up at Cambridge and seeing out my twenties, I had some unusually vivid and rather macabre dreams, not unlike the German films I was enjoying then. But towards the middle of the 1920s, when life itself was like an evil dream, the nights offered me nothing between a fearful brooding and a blessed forgetfulness. Not a single dream returns to me. The 1930s and my own forties were the big dreaming time. When a man reaches forty he is nearing the top of the hill he has been climbing since boyhood, and, passing the summit, he will find himself looking down instead of up, perhaps seeing far below an ancient village with its church and its graveyard. Vaguely aware of this change of direction, catching a glimpse of that village below, a determinedly unwise man may proceed to heighten and strengthen the barrier between consciousness and the unconscious, dreaming less not more. Not wise, God knows, but at least not building a blind wall, I had some nightly visitations from the creative depths of our being.

It was then there came that *Dream of the Birds*, which I certainly do not intend to describe all over again, especially after it has been often quoted and recited or read in public performances. It was then too I had my dream within a dream or, to be more exact, a tiny nightmare enclosed within a dream, which offered me, like a Turkish bath, an anteroom of rest and refreshment before and after the ordeal of maximum steam heat. Did I unknowingly create this decent arrangement, keeping the nightmare part removed and small and brief instead of plunging me straight into horror? And if I were not responsible for this, then *who was*?

I don't know. And what I don't know seems to enlarge itself every month or so, yielding dim vistas of ignorance.

No succeeding decade brought such a dream harvest as the 1930s. My fifties, sixties, seventies were sufficiently eventful from morn to midnight but offered me little or nothing worth remembering from my sleep. During recent years I seem to have been the victim of daft little worry dreams that vanish five seconds after waking. It is as if I were clerk to a lawyer or an accountant, but a clerk more than half out of his mind, perhaps far gone in drink or senility, worrying idiotically over a phrase or a sum like a dog with a dry old bone. These were quite different from the old anxiety dreams that concentrated on travel, giving you a train to catch at Paddington but distributing your luggage between Hampstead and Blackheath. I often had these dreams, chiefly I think because I did travel a lot and behind my swagger was at heart a rather nervous apprehensive traveller, always arriving early at railway stations and airports. (But often enjoying stations while always hating airports.) However, such dreams did at least bring release to anxiety and often enabled me to laugh at myself. But this much later and much longer series of niggling little worries, pedantry *Through the Looking Glass*, lunatic clerkships, brought me no relief that I could distinguish and seemed to me an irritating waste of dream time. Indeed, having entered my eighties I felt that I had long come to the end of my ration of rewarding dreams, that as a dreamer I had withered away.

I was wrong. (This piece is here to prove how wrong I was.) As I write this, it is only a few weeks since there arrived, out of the dark and against all odds, a big memorable dream, a creation instead of mere hotchpotch and mental slush, an event—a most notable event—in my dreaming life: *The Happy Dream.*

TWO

Like a good Englishman I shall begin my account of this dream with the weather. It was perfect, out of the Maytime of some mysterious dimension. The sunshine was bland and from first to last, as I well remember, there was a pleasant breeze. Nothing glittered but everything seemed to sparkle a little, rather as if this world in which I suddenly found myself had just been made —as indeed it had been. Here I was in a closer relationship with the weather than I had been throughout thirty to forty waking years. My body, we might say, was tasting the day and finding it good. It was an experience I had lost sight of along the narrowing way.

But then I was now wearing another body. I was out of the clumsy carcase, creaking and groaning with age, that takes me longer and longer to dress and undress—I who was once so quick, so deft. Bodily I had been returned to early manhood—at a guess sometime in the early twenties. I was aware of this at once, before I noticed anything happening except the new-minted golden weather. And not only that, I had acquired a youthful spirit too. This was soon proved because I found I was a member of a small group—perhaps half-a-dozen or so—about to move around without any particular plan or destination, the kind of thing that idle young men like to do and that elderly men detest, possibly because, unlike young men, they feel their time is running out and not to be wasted on vague impulses. The fact that I accepted and joined in this almost featureless ploy confirms that I had acquired with the body a genuine youthful spirit.

But—and this is the largest *But* in all these pages—I had not entirely lost myself as I am now. Behind the youthful body and spirit was the self that had lived so long and experienced so much. Yet, while knowing itself to be there, it was not detached from the other two. A current ran right through from that body tasting

[108]

the weather to that habitual old self, not only joining in but *joining on*. And what came through was not simply pleasure but a rich breadth and depth of happiness I never remember feeling before, awake or in dreams. (The sudden ecstasy I knew at the end of *The Dream of the Birds* belonged to a different order of feeling, immensely heightened but doomed to be brief, not to be lived with as I felt this new dream happiness could be—and *ought to be*.) And here I must warn the reader that the rest of my account of this dream will probably come as an anti-climax.

Perhaps it is better to explain here and now why no personal encounters and strange events should be expected. As I suggested in the previous section, an important dream of this kind, important because whatever is central in it persistently haunts the memory, is a definite creation. It is the opposite of a hotchpotch. It is designed, shaped, coloured, to make a certain impression. It might be described as the unconscious cornering consciousness. A point had to be driven home. This had nothing to do with personal relations, so I was only vaguely aware of other people, not a face nor a voice remaining in my memory. There were no striking events, no challenges to courage or endurance, because the dream was not concerned with such matters. What it was concerned with, what it presented at the first moment, was this glorious atmosphere, immediately radiating happiness, so memorable that I could not forget it if I tried. It would have been more or less the same if I had seen nobody and gone nowhere. What was at the core of the experience was the sense of myself both young and old. What this Happy Dream celebrated so richly was the defeat of Time.

I realized that our small group, whose faces and voices have escaped me, was drifting round Cambridge. I knew it was Cambridge, as one does in dreams, without recognizing any signs of the actual place—no colleges, no river, no bridges and 'backs'. And why should Cambridge come floating into this great flood of happiness? I was grateful to it, for it accepted me when I had no scholarship to offer it, only three wound stripes and a few early pieces in print; but I never felt at home in the place and never looked back on my three years there with the faintest glimmer of sentiment. But is there a clue to be found in quite a different direction, with a leap forward from 1921-2 to 1947-8? It was then, through Unesco at first, that I was brought into frequent contact with Jacquetta Hawkes, afterwards—and there was a stroke of luck, by Heaven!—to be my wife. Now Jacquetta was the daughter of a famous Cambridge scientist, born in Cambridge, brought up and educated there, a Cambridge girl if there ever was one. So is this why, floating on this wonderful tide of happiness, I came first to Cambridge?

I seem to remember that our little aimless group wandered down some side-streets, but then we came to something that made me linger behind the others. It was an enormous kind of shed, as big as a hangar, with one end open to the street. An orchestra was rehearsing just inside the entrance, and beyond it, hard to see and impossible to hear, there seemed to be a number of ensembles also at rehearsal. In the dream this did not strike me as an impossible arrangement; it was only when recalling this strange visit to Cambridge that I told myself that no musicians in their senses could have tolerated that crowded shed. There is of course some symbolism here, but its meaning and significance escape me. I am adequate only on symbols that appear in other people's life and work. There are some novels of mine—and *Lost Empires* stands out among them—that carry a load of symbols, I gather from what other people have told me; and I doubt if I spotted one of them myself. But then this is as it should be. Highly conscious symbolism—sticking the things in like currants into a cake—won't do at all. They should arrive like that musical giant shed in a dream Cambridge.

Then it wasn't Cambridge. I was in the Isle of Wight, though there was nothing I could see to remind me of the island, where I had lived for many years. I was still one of a small group, though I feel sure it was not the Cambridge group. We were on our way up to a castle, on a broad path that had occasional shallow steps, grassy rather than stony. A girl was walking immediately ahead of me, the first I had seen in this dream. I never exchanged a word with her nor even saw her face, and the view I had of her rather sturdy but shapely figure, one of the group but with no companion at the moment, did not suggest any particular girl I had ever known. But the sight of her, I remember, brought a new glow of feeling to the happiness that had been there from the first. Woman had arrived. Not my woman, no woman I wanted personally, but *Woman*, essential femininity, heightening the delight of that bland sunshine and the pleasant breeze and the sparkle of a world that might have been newly created.

This I remember almost as if it had happened at lunchtime today. And that is all I remember. We went on climbing, without effort or weariness, but we never reached that castle on some Isle of Wight in an unknown dimension. (You take the symbolism: I pass.) I woke up, but without any regret immediately, for the extraordinary happiness the dream had brought me, that magical current that had passed through the youthful body and spirit to warm and illuminate this old mind, remained with me, almost in its full effect, for several waking hours. It has haunted me ever since.

There was nothing solid, nothing to live with, nothing real about that Cambridge I could not recognize or that thin sliver, reduced to one path, of the Isle of Wight. They were merely small contributions from the scenic department of the dream theatre. My companions were not persons but only figures in a frieze. The dream's events, as I have shown, were of little importance. What was all-important, what was real, was the great happiness I felt. If that was not real, then I am not real. We must remember too that this happiness began with the dream, continued—perhaps with an extra glow—throughout it, and refused to fade completely hours after waking. Indeed, after weeks, though it is now further off and smaller, squeezed by the pressure of ordinary living, it has not entirely left me yet. But something else has happened. It has brought me a number of questions, rising like so many curved snakes, that I may not be able to answer but I feel I cannot ignore. A dream at once so strange and so memorable comes with a challenge. I may not be the right man to meet it fairly and squarely, but I would be a coward if I pretended it wasn't here, staring me in the face.

THREE

To deal with this challenge, it seemed to me, I would have to approach and then consider this dream on various different levels, no matter how far this might take me. But before I arrived at the first acceptable level, I appeared to be arguing about my dream with a Dr Consensus, a rather aggressive type.

Dr Consensus said it was childish. I replied that as my old age played an important part in the dream, 'childish' would not do—except of course as something to throw at me. He said the dream offered me an obvious impossibility. We cannot be old and young at the same time. The dream merely staged an absurd wish. It was a good example of a weakly foolish kind of dreaming. He didn't go on to suggest I was entering my second childhood, but he made me feel that the notion was somewhere round the corner. And to all this I brought up a barrage of replies.

In these days, I said, when the most advanced scientists are beginning to wonder where they are, even a Dr Consensus ought to be a bit careful about playing *impossibility* as if it were an ace of trumps. We seem to live, I reminded him, in a universe that is not only very large but also very strange, probably up to almost anything. (Those black holes, for example.) We are not very sure even of what is going on all round us. We must exist in ordinary time and space and yet things happen that don't seem to be aware of that fact. Some of yesterday's impossibilities now begin to look like possibilities. Again, this weakly foolish dream brought me a flood of happiness that shines yet in my memory. Nothing weak, nothing foolish, about the depth and height of that feeling.

Somewhere down there, fumbling in the dark of the mind, I had won the jackpot. Dr Consensus was not going to have that. It was not an odd something in me that insisted upon it, but an odd something in him desperately anxious to deny the experience.

How can I say this? Because otherwise he would not have been so eager to take the wonder, the magic, the mystery, out of my dream. He would not have wanted to scale it down, to flatten it, to blanket its glowing hues, its tone, its tang, and then rush it into the colourless, flavourless world we are so busy trying to create, to bore ourselves so long and hard that Death can seem a welcome visitor. Goodbye, Dr Consensus!

The first level worth considering can be called Jungian. Jung believed that the unconscious—his the deepest and most commodious of its kind—acted as a balancer or corrector of consciousness. If a man's consciousness were one-sided, then his unconscious would be other-sided. Though a heightened and broadened consciousness was the ultimate aim, some guidance, mainly by way of dreams, was needed from the unconscious and its ancient and enduring archetypes. No advice delivered in our ordinary language could come from down there, which dealt in visual signs and symbols and the strange stuff of dreams. But why should the unconscious be capable of advising and guiding the ego, always so busy, so inquisitive? Here I will avoid the mystical department, where a door in the most remote depths might open to reveal God blazing away. I will assume it is all a question of experience. At the most my ego's experience goes back 80 years. The experience of the unconscious, not personal but collective, goes back 800, 8000, 80,000, 800,000 years. So it is entitled to tell us a thing or two.

What did it tell me in that dream? First, it must be understood what had been going on before the dream arrived. My aged mind seemed lively enough—though there I might have been flattering myself—but feeling of any depth and richness seemed to have withered away. The springs of generous emotion appeared to have dried up. I felt less and less and might feel nothing more until a senile self-pity took possession of me and kept me maudlin and tearful at the fireside. Now into this desert of emotion the dream brought a great and astounding flood of intense happiness. Little else was there, as I have already explained, but then what *was* there was exactly what was needed. By being attached to a youthful body and spirit my mind, aged, darkening, growing colder, was immediately and magically warmed and illuminated.

Now I need not have felt that. I might have told myself that this was a silly dream, that I had no desire to go wandering about with a group of young idiots, and that I ought to wake up as soon as possible and get on with my sensible grumbling ordinary life. But because I reacted as I did, the dream suggested that there still existed in me the potentiality to enjoy something like a rich warm feeling of happiness. I am not going to pretend that that is what I am now enjoying, even though the dream haunts me still. But I am not quite the same as I was before, and a certain possibility, rather like a distant luminous cloud, persists in my imagination. So far as the unconscious can have an intention, was this it? Did the dream carry a message that I have only half-understood? Possibly, possibly not. But this is the end of my exploration of it on the Jungian level.

We might risk a glimpse of a kind of mezzanine level, sanctified by the Christian Church. Why not? If a woman had been visited by this dream, she might have cried afterwards: 'Utter bliss—oh, Heavenly!' And surely we could use a few ideas for Heaven? Hell we are capable of furnishing and decorating at any time, without any inspiration from above or below. No lack of ideas there. 'Leave it to us,' we might shout to Satan. Not so with Heaven. We feel so uncertain about our continued happiness up there that secretly we prefer cosy Limbo. We cannot look forward to all that harp work and Choral Society festivals. It may be all very well for angels because, in spite of their impressive appearance, there is something silly about them. And I for one shrink from a God whose only idea is to hear Himself endlessly praised. To meet 'loved ones' again—yes, certainly, but we must be able to enjoy a few common activities, and nothing has been suggested. Hymns are no help here. And indeed, where do we look? While Hell is never short of an idea, is doing a roaring trade and is probably already over-booked, there is something thin, chilly and tedious about our notions of Heaven.

So what about my dream? No, this is not an immodest suggestion. I am thinking only about something that could happen in distant outskirts, far away from the divine Albert Hall, just a little heavenly arrangement perhaps for newcomers. Dr Consensus and his kind could not object to it as an impossibility, for up there the souls must at least be freed from the slavery of passing time, so that a young body and spirit could easily be attached to an experienced mind. I merely offer it as one idea when there does seem to be shortage of ideas to create happiness. Yes, Your Holiness, My Lord, only for remote areas that probably receive numbers of newcomers, dismayed at first, after a wretched old age, to discover that Death has not put them to sleep for ever. It might work, you know: they really might feel they were in Heaven.

While we move from the mezzanine to the next floor, the Time Department, I could share a fancy that has sometimes entertained me. I have been put in charge of Human-Death-and-Destiny. I then decide that Death should offer people not what they don't want but all that they most urgently desire. In short, the Death-Wish comes true. Thus, if a man is sick and tired of life—as so many seem to be—and wants it extinguished, then it is immediately blotted out for him. But there cannot be any cheating. He cannot be 'enjoying the long rest' his relatives tell us he is doing. To do this he would have to be conscious and then he would weary of his long rest but would not be able to escape from it— a nightmare existence.

There would be no happy ending for the villains. A Hitler, for example, would go on to conquer Russia, then all Asia, and would be trying to plan the invasion of North America. But his voice would be gone after too many screaming exhortations; his headquarters would be a mile underground; extermination camps would be multiplied monstrously; plots against his life would be endless; he would soon have created for himself a hell of a time. All the haters would go on hating without stint until they searched in vain for anybody who could even begin to like them. The murderers, the torturers, the sadists, would indulge themselves on such a scale that soon they would feel satiated and wonder what to do with themselves. The point here is of course that while goodness offers enormous variety, evil has certain limitations. A further point is that if wishes are coming true, we must be very careful what we wish.

I seem to remember Dr Consensus, giving me up, muttering something about fairy tales. Obviously he knew nothing about them, hadn't looked at one for years. I might have broken a rule and quoted to him a speech that occurs in a new play of mine:

'But you've missed the point of fairy tales, Ann. The people who live happily ever afterwards are only those who've passed all the tests, who defied giants and dragons and sorcerers and witches. You can have magic wishes in a fairy tale, but if you make the wrong wish, you might be changed into a frog or a stone image—or vanish for ever. I tell you, it's a more searching and harder life in fairy tales than it is slopping and yawning about in a welfare state, waiting to sit through *Match of the Day*.'

Returning to my fancy about the real Death-Wish coming true, there might be only a few who urgently desired a more fruitful and rewarding kind of life. And by that I don't mean they would be asking a Red Indian neighbour in the Hereafter to put them in touch with a spiritualist circle in Bromley. I mean something quite different, as I hope we shall see.

But we are now in the Time Department. Clocks of all shapes, sizes and ages are ticking away, like so many noisy ants busy destroying the very foundations of this life. No dream, even of the most foolish sort, could find its way in here. Dreams don't go to work with this clock time. They don't recognize its existence. They wouldn't know how to function if they were clamped into its single dimension. Even in their ordinary structure, when they are offering us all kinds of nonsense we forget at once, they leap around, in and out of this solitary track, defying and confusing our familiar time order. (They behave as our memory so often does.) Nor is that all. On rare occasions they can detonate the whole logic of clock time by taking us into a future that is not supposed to exist. They show us, let us say, the sharp image of a lame man with red hair, and then on Tuesday week we run into him for the first time. (I have had these precognitive dreams and happen to have read descriptions of many hundreds of them, and it appears to be fairly certain that their images are sharper and more easily remembered than those of ordinary dreams.) With all this in mind, we don't loiter in the Clock-Time Department but move up to another floor.

Call this if you like the Crackpot Department, where dreams flourish. Let us assume—if only to approach my dream on another and final level—that Time has not simply one dimension —but three. Or that the universe does not stop at the fourth dimension but has a fifth and sixth. Let the fourth dimension be clock time, passing time, world time. Let the fifth be enduring time, in which anything that has happened goes on happening: an order of being sometimes called Eternity, which must not be mistaken for endless passing time. Then let there be a sixth dimension, the realm of creative time, in which what can be found in the fourth and fifth dimensions can be rearranged and brought to new life by a powerful impulse to create new life. (Here in this sixth dimension—or the depth of the cube of Time— is the workshop of the great masters.) And given this, if a dream be the creator, then that 'obvious impossibility' denounced by Dr Consensus becomes a possibility.

No doubt it will surprise some readers if I declare here and now that I believe in reason. It is however a reason that casts a far wider net than the severely rational or logical positivism. (I cannot *prove* how wildly happy I was in my dream, but it will be a rash man who tells me to my face that both the dream and this essay are loads of rubbish.) Some things are reasonable; others are not. It would be absurdly unreasonable, for instance, to deny the death of the body. But to my mind it would also be unreasonable to suppose that the end of a body involves the complete extinction *of a person*. We assume, in a fairly reasonable fashion, that a person isn't a body but *has* a body. It is true we also assume that a person must have a body. But do we know enough about death and bodies, down to their molecules and atoms, to state with certainty that a person could not acquire, not having been obliterated by death, another and different kind of body. However, at the risk of seeming unreasonable, I must point out that we know fairly well a body quite different from the one we habitually cart around with us.

This is the body we know in our dreams. It has its limitations; there can be no doubt about that. But it also possesses some advantages. It can move from room to room without hindrance and friction, apparently gliding through walls. It can travel faster than the fastest jet. It can cope—though not always, I admit—with fantastic experiences. Living with it we seem to be free from most minor injuries or petty annoyances. (Unless of course the dream itself is about such things.) With its help we can float across and observe magical landscapes. At the worst it doesn't *bore us* as our ordinary bodies so often do. And while we are with it, we can be gripped and shaken by feelings that reach us from some unknown source. Their range is as impressive as their force, from horror and terror through wonder to sudden joy. Is there any possible connection between this body we have in dreams and the kind of body we might acquire after death? After all, being a reasonable man, I don't know.

Do I know on which level we should approach and then explain my dream? The only one I definitely reject is that of mere hotchpotch, of ragbag, of mental garbage disposal. Both experience and reason seem to support me here. Such dreams never remain to haunt the memory. This has to be another kind of dream. It might have been created as a warning message from the unconscious to consciousness, from some unknown depth of ancient wisdom to the foolish ego. It might—though I have not much hope of this—be a glimpse of Heaven, somewhere along its outskirts, which could include another Cambridge, another Isle of Wight. It might be accepted as an adventure in the third dimension of Time or the sixth dimension of the universe. Or could it—and this question has just flashed across my mind—be all of these, refusing to cancel out one another? Again, I don't know.

What I do know is this. Ordinary living, with all its abrasive demands, its dream-diminishing tactics, has been hard at work during these past few weeks. (Am I not a reasonable and fully responsible man still, age or no age?) Yet though it has all retreated a little, its images not as sharp and bright as they were, the happy dream has not gone. I can still be enchantingly aware of that bland sunshine and that pleasant breeze, of that youthful body and spirit with which I encountered this newly-made world, of that magical happiness which never left me but began to deepen and glow as we climbed the path to the castle I never saw. How can we still say 'Only a dream'? This one brief dream towered above and outshone all the recent events of my old age. It has been the greatest gift that has lately come my way.

SOME
AFTERTHOUGHTS

To answer that we must briefly return to the Essay text. There I described myself as a nervous apprehensive traveller. I didn't mean that I am in a fearful state about the journey itself. Not at all. The truth is, I am always nervous and apprehensive about *missing* the plane or train, so that I always insist upon arriving early, dreading any last-minute rush. (Moreover, years ago, I missed the Barcelona–Paris Express, and condemned myself to catching local trains all over France, paying more and more, first for frustration and then for increasing boredom. A lesson, I can tell you!) So, as I like to arrive early, I am referring to railway stations and large airports in terms of waiting in them. The official procedure may be more impersonal in stations, but the places themselves seem to be far closer to ordinary warm human living. They exist in a far better atmosphere. The large airports will give you a name, and will cry or boom it out if you have not arrived in the plane; but even so they exist in an atmosphere withering to true personality, an atmosphere in which you are no longer a fellow human being, *a man and a brother.*

So I feel, as I wait, that a huge machine, some triumph of technology, has taken over. It is quite a polite and even considerate machine, aware of your name and wanting you to start your journey. But this is so that a list can be properly checked. The complicated machine has to function properly. You now exist, as you wait, in a conditioned air that begins to be diminishing and desiccating. You are less than half your usual self, and the people all round you in the great lounge hall look at least as bad as you feel, many of them so drooping and mournful. Even the brassy drinking type—another for the road, old boy—are clearly overdoing character parts. Even if there is music, it is machine music, provided by some distant orchestra of robots. The monstrously amplified announcements—*Ruritania Airways announce the departure, etc.*—never varying in tone, offer us no breath of life, no hint of fellow-feeling. The machine has spoken. The uniformed girls, trim and smiling, who conduct us here and there, seem far removed from the delicious wayward creatures their boy-friends know as girls. The bus to the plane or that walk across the tarmac are not warmed by any laughter or even smiles. We might be on

[124]

our way to some kind of concentration camp. We are in the grip of the machine.

We can give a guess at the way the world has been going if we consider transport down the years. Notice its send-off. If the old prints are to be believed—and I think they are—the stagecoaches left their inns with trumpets, bugles, horns sounding, all manner of blown kisses and wavings, inn loungers cheering and urchins turning somersaults. The journey itself might be uncomfortable but it always started in fine style. The same might be said of most ships, moving off after a wealth of incidents, last drinks, fond farewells, cheers galore and perhaps a band playing. (I often departed in ships during the '20s and '30s, when I could still afford to pay the passages. The best send-off of all was when I sailed from San Francisco to Tahiti in 1931—such a rich warm scene, so many songs, flowers, smiles and tears, shoutings and wavings, with a billowing carpet of petals following us!) Even to board a long-distance train, some noble express, was to take part in an event, with the platform filled with people blowing last kisses and waving us away, as if we were bound on an adventure. And now where have we got to? In airports no last farewells; no flowers, no tears, no smiles. Lost in the machine, glum and silent, we are herded to the tarmac and the most recent example of advanced technology, which will take us to another airport just like the one we left. The lively event, the warmth, the fun, have gone. It is, at heart, a deadly bore.

II

ABOUT MY EXPERIENCE. I am rather given to boasting, as my loved ones have told me more than once. But even they would allow me to declare that my experience has been unusually long, thick, and rich. It is not to be despised even biologically: I have been married three times, have five children, fifteen grandchildren, and at least—as I write here—one great-grandchild. (Believing, most of the time, that there are too many people already in the world; though there are some good genes at work in this family.) Not offering much charm myself, still I may be said to have lived a charmed life. In the First War I was wounded, buried alive, and partly gassed. In the Second, broadcasting through various blitzes, I was busy dodging—or hoping to dodge—landmines, high explosive bombs, incendiaries. Indeed, when in a boastful mood, I claim that everything lethal has been hurled at or dropped on me except of course nuclear bombs, and nobody can say I haven't denounced *them*. (Am I a hero? Not a bit. Too much imagination. Three-fifths coward, afraid even of the bullocks in our pasture and of any large dog I don't know.) Though supposed to be bravely outspoken, sometimes I fancy I am a bit short of *moral courage*. But certainly not short of experience.

I sold my first piece to a London periodical in 1910, and still have my eye on an editor or two, even if they think I am now in an old man's home. I have not only written a lot, I have written *too much*. (All the same, a man I don't know, recently reviewing me, said I had written *three masterpieces*. Very well, pull a face, but how many have *you* written?) Boasting on, I have taken curtain calls, wreaths and all, in far, far more theatres than any drama critic in this country has ever seen or—I am ready to bet—will ever see. I have been a best-seller and a worst-seller. (All experience.) In 1940 I was one of the most popular men in the country, and about ten years later, judging by the way everything I did was clobbered, one of the most unpopular men in the country. (Experience again.) Once a junior clerk in a wool office, without any Establishment influence and backing, I have been president of this, chairman of that, and have raised my voice, not unlike that of an angry Bradford wool-sorter, at various international conferences.

Though never concentrating on radio (except during the Second War) and television, I go back a long time in these media. I was on radio in the old Savoy Hill days. I spoke on TV in the later 1930s, when nobody outside this country knew that television existed. In spite of all the writing I have done, I have delivered lectures from Iowa to Athens, from Stockholm to Southern Chile, where students crowded in because they thought I was Elvis Presley. I have been bored in Samarkand and amused in Pittsburgh. I have drunk coffee and whisky in the howling dark of an Aleutian island, and have seen a line of great golden kangaroos come leaping out of a wood near Alice Springs. I have submitted to 108 in the shade in the Sudan and forty below in Canada. I have seen the Taj Mahal, the temples in Cambodia, and Abu Simbel on the Nile. I have starred for ten nights in a West End theatre. I ran a high-level chamber music festival for ten years. Among many other drolleries, I have taught an English Department in Tiflis to sing 'Old Macdonald Had a Farm', and persuaded the wives of Japanese tycoons to join me in playing the old army drinking game of 'Cardinal Puff'. Yes, yes—*Experience!* (I once owned a haunted house in the Isle of Wight.) Yes, long and thick and rich! I could go on with this, but really it's insufferable. However, I trust I have made my point.

III

ABOUT PERSONAL RELATIONSHIPS. I think the Essay makes it quite clear why I never got to know any of the people I was roaming round with, and why indeed any intrusion of personal relationships would have changed the whole character of the dream. But now I am asking myself about such relationships, searching my memory to some extent. As I poke around in there, I find much that is good and perhaps much more that is bad and distressing. Complete honesty is probably impossible in a self-examination; but I will do my best.

Apart from one or two failures, I would say that I have been successful and happy in my intimate personal relationships—those, for example, with my wife and family. This is also true of a fairly small circle of friends, most of whom I have known for many years. (But death has removed some of my oldest and closest friends—a penalty one pays for a long life. So, for instance, there is nobody alive now with whom I can share reminiscences of our life at Cambridge: Davison, Bullett, Kendon—poets all three of them—have vanished—alas!) I can say much the same of the people who have worked with or for me for any real length of time. We both respected and liked one another. A good relationship was there. Death and retirement have come breaking in, but some of it still exists today. In all of this I have been fortunate, probably receiving more rewards than I have deserved.

Now for the bad part. This is not a matter of my 'public image', largely a creation of the Press. (A chap wants an interview and you are too busy at the moment, so he suggests in print you are a cantankerous man.) But an image of sorts does come into the melancholy business, melancholy because where there might have been a decent and even rewarding personal relationship, there is nothing but misunderstanding, disappointment, a wrong idea. But now the repulsive image is entirely my own creation. It has always been my own fault, and I wretchedly suspect it has happened hundreds of times. To say I have been tactless lets me off too easily. I have been a mannerless blundering idiot, over and over and over again. Where a comfortable personal relationship might have flourished, a chance meeting ends in a desert or an icy tundra. How conceited! How ill-bred! How bloody rude! Well, that's the very last time I'll have anything to say to *him*! How can such people, crying out like that, ever be persuaded to believe that my intimate personal relationships survive the closest scrutiny?

A brief sketch of what must have happened so many times. You have read and liked something that Priestley has written, and, meeting him for the first time at some function, make haste to tell him what you feel. Does he listen carefully, look happy, smile, gracefully offer you his thanks? He does not. He scowls, makes an abrupt impatient gesture, mutters something that doesn't suggest any thanks, does a final glare and moves away. Or you are a lady at a dinner party, and, knowing how most men love to talk about their work, you ask this man Priestley what he is writing now. He stares at you; his bristling eyebrows descend ominously; then he looks somewhere else; finally he growls 'Ah've a roole not to talk about what Ah'm doing.' What a boor!

Having accused myself, I shall now proceed to excuse myself. The impatient gestures, a breach of social discipline, were almost always involuntary. It is true that for many years I was an impatient man, but there was really no arrogance in this. During many of those years, roughly between 1930 and 1950, I was carrying too heavy a load. I was doing two or three men's work. (Had I my time over again, I would take on far less.) I was impatient with myself as well as with so many other people. So much for those gestures. As for my face, it has always been treacherous. It expresses far more than I really feel, just as if it had gone on the stage to play melodrama. It can look furious when I am no more than mildly annoyed. All that staring, glowering, frowning, glaring, merely mean that it is up to its tricks again, well out of my control. It may have cost me scores of pleasant personal relationships. The people who know me well must have learnt to ignore my face, no treat even when it is behaving properly.

What about my voice then? No, it isn't also playing tricks. It happens to be naturally resonant and rumbling. (I seem to remember a passage in Rose Macaulay—rather a snob in her way—in which she said that no true gentlemen ever had such voices.) But along with this resonance and rumbling there remains a sharp trace of my original Bradford accent. Now there is something aggressive about this Bradford accent, partly due to its emphatic consonants. A Bradford (pronounced *Bratfut*) man, offering condolences to a friend who has just lost his mother, can sound as if he were making a final offer for ten bales of cross-breds. My relatives were fond of me when I was a boy, but a stranger, overhearing them greet me, would imagine they were shouting angrily. Incidentally, I don't shout. Also, not so incidentally, when I work at it I can be very persuasive.

But I have no doubt that all too often I have been tactless, overbearing, insensitive, disappointing, alienating people who might have become my friends. And for a man who *believes* in personal relationships, as I certainly do, there is nothing here to be proud of. However, this is not why, tagging along, I never got to know anybody in my Happy Dream, which was too busy showing me how *to enjoy myself* outside ordinary passing-time.

IV

ABOUT THE WEATHER. It was something like a stroke of genius to begin that dream with the weather. (Remember, I never felt that I had created that dream, which seemed to come as a gift from outside, just as a box of Partagas or a bottle of old Armagnac might arrive as a birthday present.) The golden weather was there, waiting for me. Then I was in it, tasting it, loving it. I had not felt such a rich response to weather for years. To a sedentary ageing man, the weather, unless it is really threatening, is a mere backdrop. He isn't in it, tasting it, loving it. He may just observe that it is better or worse today than it was yesterday. He would deny at once that anything less than extra-ordinary weather shaped and coloured his feelings, had any effect on him at all. Meeting another Englishman, he might mention the weather, but just as a conversational gambit. But how very rarely indeed he genuinely enjoys it! And how clever it was of that happy dream to compel me to taste and relish its weather!

This was designed to please me. It was sunny without being really warm. It was sparkling without glaring anywhere. It offered me a pleasant breeze that never turned into a high wind, which I detest. There are places in the world—and I have been to one or two of them—where the wind blows hard every day; and this I would find unendurable very soon. Equally unendurable after a short time are those places, like Lima in Peru, that are very warm but have no sunshine, existing in a grey sticky haze and damp underclothes. And to tell the truth, though I grumble about English weather, I am not fond of those places that offer you exactly the same kind of day, however bright, month after month: so many boring tourists' paradises, for whose sake hordes of men have toiled or swindled. I prefer spending my life in changeable weather, not scraping and saving nor cheating to domicile myself in a bland monotony.

However, I have felt a touch of shame these last few days. One of my grumbles has been that too many English days really have no character at all. They neither spread rain over the fields nor bring out the sun to dry them. They have no colour. They offer us a uniform featureless greyness. Now I have been re-reading, after a long interval, that huge *Wolf Solent*, by that equally huge sprawling genius, John Cowper Powys. (Incidentally he explores the difficult frontiers, half-conscious, half-unconscious, of sexual relations far better than D. H. Lawrence ever does. But he is also capable of postponing a dramatic scene to brood for a page over a dandelion.) So what about *Wolf Solent*? Well, he finds a sort of magic and often ecstasy in these same grey days that I have often abused. This means—for there is truth behind his eloquence— that his life has been richer than mine, that I have grumbled myself into a certain poverty of experience. If I had noticed more, instead of complaining, I would have had more. All the same, I can't help remembering that Powys wrote *Wolf Solent* when he was still in America, three thousand miles from any grey days in Dorset.

The perfect weather—perfect for me, anyhow—stayed with me in the dream. I was conscious of it, savouring it, from first to last. And, in the Essay, after talking about tasting the day and finding it good, I go on to say, 'It was an experience I had lost sight of along the narrowing way.' In other words, I had this feeling about the weather just because part of me was young again. But is it true? I can recall my early twenties but I don't remember having this special feeling about the weather. I enjoyed what I *did* with the weather, so to speak, going for long walks or playing games, but I don't remember anything like this weather-tasting, just as if I had opened a bottle of wine. To arrive at such moments I would have to return to childhood and some bright mornings at the seaside, with the sun on the seaweed and dipping into those mysterious pools that children love. And all this was well outside the scope of my dream.

I think that dream-weather was a very artful creation. It was not there simply because part of me was young again. It was there because another part of me was still old, catching at youth and all that it was promised. And so, chiefly among what the old man thought youth was promised was perfect weather, a sparkling day, never too warm, and a pleasant breeze that never turned into a high wind.

V

ABOUT CAMBRIDGE. The Essay explains why a rather strange visit to Cambridge pops up in my Happy Dream. But I think a more realistic Cambridge, which I left without any regret fifty-four years ago, would stand a fairly stout Afterthought. Not that I have anything to resent. Cambridge treated me very decently when I was up there. Strictly speaking, I didn't deserve to be there at all, having no claims to scholarship, with my school-days long gone, working in an office before spending four-and-a-half years in the army, and an outsider, an uncouth Northerner if there ever was one. Yes, going there was a stroke of luck, even if I was a trifle unlucky in the college I was assigned to, for Trinity Hall was devoted to the Law, rowing and an expensive kitchen if you could afford to patronize it. I couldn't; I wanted (then and since) to have nothing to do with the Law; and I was in no shape to start rowing. The good friends I made were all in other colleges; I had only one at the Hall, who had the very literary name of Byron-Scott but was actually a musician; and he and I used to play duets, chiefly arrangements of Haydn symphonies, in which I was never given a shot at the treble. However, I had these good friends. Writing for the *Cambridge Review* and occasionally for some London periodicals, and publishing a little book, *Brief Diversions*, that had longer and more admiring London reviews than it deserved to have, I became some sort of character in the place. Also I came to know and like Quiller-Couch, who asked me to stay on to lecture and coach. But when I told him I had decided to go to London and risk free-lancing there, he said he had done exactly the same thing. I was married by that time, a child was on its way, I had only fifty pounds in the world; but I was ready to leave Cambridge.

The truth was, I had never felt really happy there, never even felt cosily at home. The University itself wasn't to be blamed: it had done its best for me, even though it has given me only sour or blank looks ever since I left it. The trouble was that I had gone up there at the wrong age, in my middle twenties. It was all very well for these shining-faced freshmen, newly released and promoted from school, all happy and busy buying college ties and blazers and tobacco jars with the college arms on them. It was all very well for the mature men, the dons, returning to their lecture rooms or labs. I belonged to neither group, not fowl, not fish. I certainly didn't lack experience of a sort, very grim some of it, but it played no part in the Cambridge scene. I didn't go there to enjoy that scene, as the kids or the dons did; I wanted to pick up the pieces of my life, after so much army. All the rum old rules and regulations, which the kids thought a great lark, seemed to me at my age a lot of damned nonsense, to be mostly ignored. Finally, I had to exist on an ex-officer's grant of £120 a year, and as I was determined not to ask my parents for any subsidy, I had to live at Cambridge very frugally indeed. In my second year, living out in digs, I ate so many boiled eggs (very cheap, that year) that I have never properly enjoyed them since. I paid my way in the vacations by writing and giving lectures to schools. But I had to go very carefully during term time. In those days— and I don't know what happens now—it was the Cambridge fashion to provide monster teas, crammed with muffins and crumpets and fancy cakes, and I remember how it irritated me to see men I knew, round about four o'clock, carrying fat bags of confectionery. And I never provided anybody with those Cambridge breakfasts of buttered eggs from the kitchen. I lived a spare, inhospitable existence, totally unsuited to my temperament.

Moreover, neither the weather nor the environment brought any pleasure. I have been both colder and hotter in Cambridge that in any other English town. I arrived in October 1919 during a coal strike, and I well remember sitting in my overcoat, in a room like a refrigerator, trying to read books that shook in my chilled grasp. Yet I took my first tripos exam in what seemed to me a May heatwave, when my dripping hands stuck to the paper and my writing, never a good feature, looked more illegible than ever. Again, brought up in hill country, I couldn't enjoy the Fens and those enormous depressing fields they offered me. I took walks, just for exercise, and exercise is all I got from them. Again, as far as I was concerned, Cambridge wasn't on the way to any-where else. Though not far from London, it was a remote ter-minus. In this respect, it was completely unlike Oxford, the gateway to the pleasantest parts of England. You went to Cam-bridge to acquire knowledge and to cope with enormous teas and bad dinners. You could go to Oxford for any ten of fifty good reasons. Beyond it were Bath and Wells and the Cotswolds. Beyond Cambridge were Diss and Siberia.

I ought to have gone to Oxford if it would have accepted me. (Though socially I would have been even further out.) More would have been happening there. More people would have been passing through, perhaps even more editors and publishers. No doubt it would have been *worldly*, even though it, and not Cam-bridge, has been the home of lost causes. But even so, I think the atmosphere of the place would have pleased me more. Because it is so grimly situated, lost in its savage Fens, not really on the way to anywhere, a remote temple of knowledge, Cambridge has a lot of dons, especially away from the sciences, who are not definitely arrogant but are not quite with the rest of us as men and brothers—inclined to be dry and suspicious, rather as if their fathers and uncles used to be with the Inland Revenue. I shall be told, because I don't know for myself, that Oxford produces too many social or religious snobs, members of Cabinets and gossip columnists. Perhaps if I had gone there, I might have retired, on a handsome pension, as a former Minister of Typical Develop-ments.

Not so long ago, a carefully directed TV programme showed me a Cambridge as far removed from the one I knew as Tahiti. When I was up, 1919–22, most of us lived like honest monks, all the more so because it was hard to get a proper bath. This other Cambridge was all sex and showing-off. The girls were not only invading men's rooms but were dropping their skirts before they had hardly closed the doors. None of that old stuff—arguing late over beer and pipes about idealism and materialism, the indi-

[136]

vidual against the State; but instant skirt-dropping and bed work. But the odd thing about these girls at Cambridge, so eager to grant their ultimate favours, was that after making love, no love seemed to have been made, for instead of being at least sleepily affectionate they seemed to be tetchy and quarrelsome. Did a certain Cambridge atmosphere, turning so many dons towards dryness and suspicion, gather and thicken over all those beds? Would it have been much better at Oxford?

VI

ABOUT THAT ENORMOUS MUSIC SHED. There was at least one full orchestra, together with any number of *ensembles* all rehearsing different works, in this vast shed wide open to the street. It could only have been a symbol. But of *what*? Even if only part of its meaning could be extracted, what was the dream telling me? At this time of writing, I haven't yet posed this question to any close and sensitive friend. And such a one is necessary for any interpretation. It is my experience that a man cannot begin to explain the symbols found in his own work. He may not even know they are there. But why this enormous shed and all this preposterous rehearsing at the same time, a situation that any sensible musician would have denounced at once? Was this really about music or about something quite different? At the moment I haven't the least notion.

A fair number of critics, discussing work of mine, have called their readers' attention to my appreciation and knowledge of music. They have flattered me, and would have done better to direct attention to my appreciation and knowledge of human nature. I have always been vaguely musical, but I wouldn't put it any higher and stronger than that. The most I can claim is that during one brief period in my youth I did try to understand harmony and counterpoint; but soon gave it up, being always disinclined to study, having an indolent mind except when actually writing. Certainly at one time I attended a lot of concerts, and I heard a number of masters of the art both in public and in private. I was also a fairly early gramophone enthusiast, and as records got better and better I acquired a modest collection of them. Not so very long ago, returning from my afternoon work I would constantly listen to records, often keeping on with one composer. (I have a fine record-player with two majestic loudspeakers.) I did this, with occasional late-evening performances, for years.

Now I have stopped. I never attend a concert. Apart from a few Mozart piano concertos, I never listen to records. A man in his eighties might be forgiven for listening to music when he ought to be doing something else. (Incidentally, I have never believed in background music, as an accompaniment to that something else; though I have known writers who actually worked with the gramophone or radio churning away.) But now in my eighties I have moved away from music. If and when I return from a walk, usually quite short, I still spread myself on the big sofa in my study, but instead of listening to records I light pipe after pipe and wander into some reverie. For some reason I can't fathom I want hardly any music, don't seem to be in need of it any longer. I am not proud of this; rather ashamed of it, in fact; and I can't pretend to understand what has happened.

I will try one guess at that enormous shed, with those hundreds of musicians making so many different sounds. Was it a protest against atonality and twelve-note composition? Was it a defence of the octave, to which both my ear and my mind are attuned? (My mind because in several theories of the universe the octave plays an important part.) Why had our noble old friend to be ruthlessly torn apart, roared down, squeaked down, all for a new ideology? Certainly, men of notable talent have done this, but a man may have a lot of talent and yet march off in the wrong direction. And there has been an awful lot of this during my adult lifetime, with fashion and all the smarter people cheering along the way. But while some of what has been produced may have compelled our reluctant admiration, how much of it has reached our affection?

I have sometimes thought that round about 1910 something peculiar—perhaps rather sinister—happened in the inner worlds of youngish men of talent, even genius. As if to prepare them for an outer world they wouldn't like. As if to set their teeth on edge in advance. We know very well that men of highly original genius have had to create their own audiences, their work at first being treated with contempt and derision. Shakespeare, a very popular dramatist, escaped most of this, but not a Rembrandt or a Beethoven, a Turner or a Wagner. But since about 1910— though you may fix your own date—something different has happened. It is as if artists, however distinguished, somehow failed to win the enduring affection of the great mass of ordinary people, as if *real art* remained private and never became really public, welcomed with delight almost everywhere. Aesthetes and ideological critics took over, but the crowds stayed away. Rembrandt and Turner can pack their exhibitions, but not the abstract men, the action painters, and the rest. Beethoven and Wagner can fill the Festival Hall, but not the atonal or twelve-note masters, though they have been around for some time now. And so it goes on. Did something peculiar happen round about 1910? And does my enormous music shed come into this? I don't know.

my small son (Tom) greeted the old lady with a comical stiff bow. What then is the possible connection between the film, *The Great Gatsby*, and Queen Victoria? The answer is that the editor of one made his bow to the daughter of the other.

After the war I moved westward and upward to a house called Brook Hill, a kind of Edwardian 'folly', though magnificently situated. From below it looked colossal, and coach drivers, stopping down there on 'mystery tours' announced that it had about ninety bedrooms. (Actually it was very shallow and would barely house my family.) All my happiest memories cluster round that house. It had a fairly large panelled hall that was wonderful for the chamber music we had every September, when we also picked pounds and pounds of mushrooms in neighbouring fields or up on the down. To watch the entrancing view emerge from the golden mists; then to pick mushrooms all afternoon; then in the evening to listen to the Brahms Clarinet Quintet: we were halfway to Heaven. We also had a little terrace, within easy reach of the kitchen and dining-room; and there, when the day was all sunlight and blue air, we would enjoy our drinks and lunch on seabass freshly caught. I remember Neville Cardus, among others, staying with us on a bright summer week-end, and after a few hours of it saying slowly to me, 'It's like a dream.' And now it seems to me like a dream too, though not more than twenty years have passed. But though we do our best here, what with one daunting circumstance and another, more taxes, higher prices, fewer friends still alive, we seem to live almost like exiles.

Not that life on the island hadn't its drawbacks. A winter fog could cut you off from the mainland for days. Again, the house itself might be lost in thick mists for half a week. Then occasionally there were furious south-western gales, trying to howl and scream the place down. Finally, the island was becoming too popular, so that, returning from London in the holiday season, you would have to wait in long queues to catch a ferry. (It was a combination of these snags that finally defeated us, driving us away, though now and then I still regret our move. But I am told —for I have never been back—that the island is more popular than ever and has been considerably 'developed'—and into *what?*) However, during our time at Brook Hill the West Wight we knew best was still unspoilt. It was bounded to the north by Newport, then a fine old county town in miniature, our dwarf metropolis. Then our way went past Carisbrooke to Freshwater and up to the high down and a sight of the Needles. (On fine Sunday mornings we used to march our guests over heath and downland to Freshwater Bay, sit outside the pub there, where I believe George Morland used to paint, and give them *Dog's Nose*, an old mixture of gin and draught ale, not intended for the sedentary.) Our southern boundary mark was probably the lighthouse at St Catherine's Point, and it was a late-night visit to the lighthouse, to watch bird-ringing, that brought me that dream of the Birds.

Except for seaside resorts along the East Coast, the rest of the island was sufficiently picturesque and offered you some fine old buildings, but our end of it had a special quality of its own. There was something else, over and above its great cliffs, coloured bays, the wonderful high downs, that seemed to belong to magic. There was a bonus from some unknown dimension. Or it began to make you feel after a time that you were entranced in a waking dream. Perhaps the poets helped here. Yes, the poets, all within our triangle. There was Keats, beginning *Endymion* at Carisbrooke. There was Tennyson, composing his favourite (and mine) *Maud* at Farringford, just beyond Freshwater. And where did Swinburne write *Atalanta in Calydon*?—why, at Shorwell, halfway between us and St Catherine's. But should I be lamenting lost magic? Here we are now, not three miles from Stratford-upon-Avon and Shakespeare. And this is his town, I have never doubted that, but, to tell the truth, he has not been around here, creating a magical atmosphere, for a long time now, and may possibly be hard at work on some planet that takes its sunlight from Sirius. But in the West Wight—at least when I was there in the 1950s— the magic still lingers. So it was entitled to make an appearance, however brief and puzzling, in my dream of happiness.

VIII

ABOUT DR CONSENSUS. I am not sure that this symbolic figure carries the right name. Behind and below him is another consensus belonging to a vast mass of ordinary people, bewildered, fearful but still hopeful, influenced by but not entirely converted by Dr Consensus, who represents here a wide and still broadening range of educated opinion of a certain sort. He it is who appears first in learned journals and then in the newspapers and on radio and TV, telling us what we ought to believe. His declared object is to spread the truth and put an end to all nonsense. His real object, I believe, is to take the magic and mystery out of everything. By the time he has explained what he has discovered, the world is duller than it was before. He does not intend to bore us—he feels he is an exciting chap, having a fair share of vanity—but continually removing more and more magic and mystery out of this life of ours, he does in fact create apathy and boredom, which can lead to feelings of frustration and finally violence. For two things cannot be denied. The first is that Dr Consensus works harder and harder and addresses larger and larger audiences. The second is that our contemporary world shows us more and more boredom suddenly erupting into violence.

Let me take an example from archaeology. We have long had a legend, which I have cherished, that once there was a very large and fertile island, perhaps almost a continent, in the Atlantic that we know as Atlantis. A host of fascinating legends cluster around it. The island-continent prospered greatly. It had a civilization of its own, the foremost of its time, when Egypt at best was one of its remote colonies. It made successful experiments with vegetables and fruit. (We are told that one of its triumphs was that neat and convenient fruit—the banana.) Its cities grew, and it built great golden temples, cared for by a

[144]

powerful and knowledgeable priesthood. But it became too rich, proud and presumptuous. It ceased to worship the gods of love and preferred dark cruel gods. It was struck by terrible earthquakes, then the ocean overwhelmed it, and it vanished utterly and became Lost Atlantis. The fascinating legends drifted on for thousands of years. But then, in our time, Dr Consensus arrived, to tell us that this was all nonsense, and that the only possible Atlantis was a small island in the Eastern Mediterranean destroyed by an earthquake. And so, at a stroke, he impoverished our imagination, leaving us with a duller world.

We have seen how Dr Consensus deals with dreams, turning what wise men (and almost all women) regarded with respect, wonder, even awe, into a nightly garbage collection, a removal of the days' mental trash. But then whenever he turns to anything that has haunted people's minds for centuries, either he banishes it altogether or makes it much smaller and duller. He is a master of what we might call 'the new miserable explanation'. Most of us have often wondered who is behind those mysterious planners giving orders to pull down charming old buildings. It is Dr Consensus, who is also responsible for the erection of those vast office blocks that nobody wants, not even the people looking for offices. In this matter, as in so many others, Dr Consensus *is not on our side*. He is determinedly against us, probably as the secret agent of some supernatural evil principle.

One of his favourite ploys is a tremendous concern for our safety. We must be on our guard against everything we really want. There, danger lies. Those brand-new medical opinions that keep cropping up in the media are largely inspired by Dr Consensus. We should like to go on eating this and drinking that, and giving them to our friends, but we ought to know that we are running a terrible risk. Why not be content—and *safe*—with raw carrots and cabbage, wheat mush and barley-water? At the same time, take care not to be an eccentric, a crackpot, a believer in all kinds of nonsense that would not survive a test in any well-equipped lab. Neither indulge your appetites nor your imagination. Look what happened to your forefathers, who did both! They all died. You may not have to die. If you have enough money, you may be kept breathing steadily in a glass case, maintained at the right temperature and guaranteed germ-proof. Write for a brochure to the Consensus Keep-Alive Co. Inc., Santa Barbara, Cal. Try for real safety—NOW!

What is Dr Consensus up to? He is doing his best to bore the hell out of us. He wants to take the variety, the colour, the juice out of everything. His idea is to make life so monotonous and safety-conscious that it is not worth living. If it is still worth an explosion, then there will be more and more huge senseless violence. This will be all the same to Dr Consensus and his diabolical employer, bent on destroying life on planet-earth. Or am I just being too fanciful? Probably. But all the same, keep an eye on Dr Consensus, and, whatever he recommends, promptly do the opposite.

IX

ABOUT HEAVEN. The passage about Heaven in the Essay is flippant and silly, and please accept my apology for it. Surely I can do better than that? I will try, though this is a difficult subject. I believe that if I worked at it, I could remember scores and scores of discussions I have had with my friends, who are all intelligent people. But I can't remember any evening when we talked about Heaven—not a single one. I may be told that this was because we didn't believe in Heaven and that any notion we might be on our way there, if we behaved ourselves, was idiotic. But are we any better off than the innocents who were certain that they and their loved ones would find themselves in Heaven? Surely not. Our later years are cheerless and theirs were not. But what about our intellectual honesty? Don't we accept the truth whereas they were deceiving themselves? But how much is that worth? After all, we aren't conducting a scientific experiment. Heaven escapes this kind of examination. Truth can't be dragged in here. The Royal Society or the British Association knows no more about our ultimate destiny than aborigines chattering round a fire. All are guessing. And indeed perhaps the aborigines are doing it better. They at least believe in some 'Great Dream Time' in which they will join their ancestors. There is more to be said for this than only believing in the undertaker and the crematorium.

The Kingdom of God is within you. But is it? I shall return to this question later. The point I want to make here is one I approached in the Essay. What we can create, without any outside assistance, is not Heaven but Hell. This we can do all on our own. We are always doing it, and have actually been cleverer at it this century than in any other. No Satan or any diabolical agency is necessary. Think of the wars, the mass murders, the

[147]

tortures, the concentration and labour camps, the terorists killing and maiming the innocent! Nor is that all. On the individual level—think of the greedy plotting, the cheating, the swindling of trusting souls, and all the men eaten by cancerous ambition! And then the families—dominated by iron-willed shrews, the husbands who come home drunk and smash the furniture, the terrified children too young to know that even misery can have an end. We need no lakes of burning sulphur or demons with pitchforks. The nearest village can rig up a hell any time. Our largest cities are probably at least one-quarter hellish. And somebody has only to press the wrong button—and half the globe will become a satanic inferno. If there are still priests who try to frighten schoolboys with official hells beyond the grave, they are out-of-date. The divine wrath hasn't to arrange anything special.

When I was a boy I had to attend Sunday morning service at our Baptist Chapel. During the week the place enjoyed itself enormously. There were jolly bazaars, teas-and-concerts, gymnastic classes, sewing meetings, jumble sales, lantern lectures, elocution recitals; and we even had our own pierrot troupe. (Instead of all that we have whole urban areas now that offer nothing but television and nervous breakdowns.) But Sunday was very different: frockcoats, best dresses, sin and suffering. Our parson, who talked me clean out of dogmatic religion at an early age, was a sufferer himself, pale and ravaged. He was addicted to long prayers in which he bullied us and then went on to bully God: *Thou knowest*, he would remind God in a sharply accusing tone. I could imagine him in an official Hell, telling people that it served them right. But I couldn't imagine him in any kind of Heaven—any more that I could imagine his sudden appearance with the Chapel pierrot troupe. I never remember seeing him around during the week. He must have stayed at home composing those long bullying prayers.

Even at the risk of seeming flippant and silly again, I must make this point about Heaven. It can't be on a do-it-yourself basis, like Hell. Even if the Kingdom is within us, and we do our best to avoid being hellish, we need some outside help to begin creating anything that could pass for Heaven. Notice how sketchy and unconvincing the official or semi-official accounts of Heaven are. If we mock them, as I did in the Essay, they have almost asked us to pull a face at them. The truth is, even with the aid of literary talent, we are much better at misery than with happiness. A pub acquaintance of mine, from long ago, Bohun Lynch, wrote a whole novel describing, I seem to remember, one supremely happy day; but it didn't work and must be entirely forgotten except by a few aged readers. No question here of edition after edition being demanded. This novel was almost instantly ignored. It happened about fifty years ago, but already then, I suspect, *we were afraid of happiness.*

This wasn't new to me, having been brought up in the West Riding. Old-fashioned nannies used to warn noisy happy children, 'You'll be crying your eyes out before the day's over'. They ought to have come from the West Riding, where a man, being congratulated on something splendid that had happened to him, would reply cautiously, 'Mustn't grumble.' That was about as far as a good West Riding man would go. Anything more than that would be 'daft'. Having been brought up in that atmosphere, I have been suspicious of happiness ever since. I feel sure that there is a catch in it somewhere. I might not be crying my eyes out soon—not being a tearful type—but I fancy I'll be getting a nasty knock or two fairly soon. (If you ever see a play of mine that opens with people being all jolly and happy, you may be sure something unpleasant is on its way to them. True, my longest and now my favourite novel, *The Image Men*, has a last chapter in which the four chief characters are gloriously happy; but then I was already old when I wrote that, and no longer gave a damn.)

Now let us consider my dream. There was in it, as I have suggested, at least just a taste of Heaven. Bliss was there, even if it didn't last long. And that was all the more remarkable because for some time before the dream came along, totally unexpected, I had been lamenting to myself the way in which feeling had begun to wither away in old age. It was as if I had had a certain capital sum of emotion and had drawn on it too often, so that now it was exhausted. To disprove this quite dramatically, the dream arrived. The feeling-bank, you might say, let me have an overdraft. So there was a brief glimpse of that bliss which we might reasonably expect in Heaven. But even here I'm afraid I must start a grumble.

Too much was missing for the dream to be accepted as a visit to Heaven. However happy I felt for the time being, I was roaming round with unknowns who never offered me a face, a voice. Where were all my loved ones and my dear friends? Without them, there was no true Heaven here. Now if I had run into them, perhaps all equally ecstatic, I would have been presented with an idea of Heaven of supreme value not only to me but also —because I would have spread the news—to a fairly large section of our bewildered and melancholy human race.

What we need so urgently now is the idea of a Heaven we could joyfully accept, together with the belief that if we behaved decently we would finally go there. That would be a piece of good news that would immediately cancel out all the bad news we get from the media. We could stand anything if we were sure of that. Notices in the *Times* would read, 'After a long illness bravely borne, Ben Snoot has gone to Heaven'. As it is, that 'long illness bravely borne' drops ice into the heart, for we imagine all those despairing visits to the hospital to see poor dear old Ben wasting away, greeting us with a ghastly little smile. And bravely borne for *what*? But if we knew that Heaven, at once splendid and sensible, was awaiting him, eager to admit him and make a fuss of him, our tears would vanish and our hearts would leap up. I tell you, what we need now is not an improvement in the National Health Service or more money all round but a much better idea of Heaven and a confident feeling we are all on our way there. We know all about Hell—it lies about us in our maturity (to improve Wordsworth)—and it is time now to give Heaven a chance. Even if, as I have said, we need help from outside, probably if we imagine boldly we are already receiving that help. And from the same mysterious source that conjures up our dreams for us.

ENVOI

I don't know how I stand with the general public, but among my family and friends I have a solid dark reputation as an inveterate grumbler. However, whatever may be said to the contrary, I don't grumble for grumbling's sake. We have plenty to grumble about, and as a nation I don't think we grumble enough. (For instance, we accept without a growl the worst public catering in Western Europe.) I offered some time ago, as an introduction to my book *Delight*, a *Grumbler's Apology*, in which I went into the whole subject; and, after all, I was writing a complete book about Delight—and how many authors have done that? However, to end this final chapter of autobiography as pleasantly as I know how, I will take a holiday from grumbling.

The truth is, that although I have known tragedy and also have my share of grievances, I have been on the whole a very lucky man. I have helped to bring up a flourishing healthy family, who always seem glad to see me. My work has gone all over the world. I have been able to write just what I wanted to write and have been handsomely rewarded for it. If I have refused various honours, it is chiefly because my name has been able to stand alone, without any fancy handles to it. Perhaps if I had to do it all over again, I would not have written so much and so many different things; but this was my own free choice, just to enjoy myself in my own way, and I was never compelled by circumstances to write on and on. I have in fact had a thoroughly good time, no doubt much better than I deserved to have. I have had to endure nothing worse than a few minor ailments, and have arrived into my eighties looking, if anything, younger and not older than my years. If I occasionally feel melancholy it is chiefly because I have outlived my closest and dearest friends. But I have many younger friends, perhaps even more women than men, always ready to flatter me a little. This is partly because they know that I have a delicious clever wife, to whom I am closely attached. And this of course has been a gigantic piece of luck.

I don't say I shall stop grumbling, not with the country in such a sad muddle and taxes and rates as they are. But I promise to avoid too many sour looks and low growls. I realize that I have had more luck than I ever deserved to have. It is time, before it is too late, that I gave the world more smiles and far fewer scowls, and began thanking God on my knees. And it is a man who knows that luck has been with him who brings this book to an end.

THE IMAGE MEN

Re-issued for the first time in one volume

J. B. Priestley wrote this novel as a single work but it was first published in separate parts in 1968 as *Out of Town* and *London End*. It is a huge comedy, sharply satirical though not sour, that ironically explores the whole image-making business. *The Image Men*, which is the author's own firm favourite among his novels, has drawn a chorus of praise from the critics:

'A very clever and funny book with real people in it.'
Iris Murdoch

'All his admirable energy, humour and steam engine narrative power ... brilliant professional skill.'
Julian Symons, *Sunday Times*

'The vigour and fluency of this latest offering put most novelists half his age to shame.'
Francis King, *Sunday Telegraph*

'The happiest Priestley for many a year.'
Ray Gosling, *The Times*

'Huge and irresistible enjoyment.'
David Haworth, *New Statesman*

'Mr Priestley handles his characters with the skill of a man who has written nearly a hundred books.'
Barry Cole, *Spectator*

'It's the kind of entertainment which I for one relish more and more.'
John Braine, *Sunday Telegraph*

'Supremely readable.'

John Raymond, *Sunday Times*

'I can't resist a creativity so exuberant that it seems not a surrogate for life, but a kind of para-experience on the same level of immediacy.'
Pat Rogers, *Observer*